THE COURAGE TO RUN

JIM RYUN
AND SONS

Regal

From Gospel Light
Ventura, California, U.S.A.

PUBLISHED BY REGAL BOOKS
FROM GOSPEL LIGHT
VENTURA, CALIFORNIA, U.S.A.
PRINTED IN THE U.S.A.

Regal

Regal Books is a ministry of Gospel Light, a Christian publisher dedicated to serving the local church. We believe God's vision for Gospel Light is to provide church leaders with biblical, user-friendly materials that will help them evangelize, disciple and minister to children, youth and families.

It is our prayer that this Regal book will help you discover biblical truth for your own life and help you meet the needs of others. May God richly bless you.

For a free catalog of resources from Regal Books/Gospel Light, please call your Christian supplier or contact us at 1-800-4-GOSPEL *or* www.regalbooks.com.

Cover photo by Rich Clarkson. Used by permission. Interior photos, unless indicated, are from the Jim Ryun Collection.

Library of Congress Cataloging-in-Publication Data
Ryun, Jim, 1947-
  The courage to run / Jim Ryun and sons.
    p. cm.
  Includes bibliographical references.
  ISBN 0-8307-3908-4 (hard cover)
  1. Christian life. 2. Ryun, Jim, 1947- 3. Runners (Sports)—United States—Biography. 4. Christian biography. I. Title.
  BV4501.3.R98 2006
  242—dc22   2006020405

1   2   3   4   5   6   7   8   9   10   /   10   09   08   07   06

Rights for publishing this book in other languages are contracted by Gospel Light Worldwide, the international nonprofit ministry of Gospel Light. Gospel Light Worldwide also provides publishing and technical assistance to international publishers dedicated to producing Sunday School and Vacation Bible School curricula and books in the languages of the world. For additional information, visit www.gospellightworldwide.org; write to Gospel Light Worldwide, P.O. Box 3875, Ventura, CA 93006; or send an e-mail to info@gospellightworldwide.org.

Coach Timmons and me. I called him "Timmie."

DEDICATION

*To Bob and Pat Timmons, without whose vision and
support I would not be the man I am today.*

*To Bernie and Clara Taylor, who pointed us to Christ
and showed a young couple so many years ago
what it was to really live.*

CONTENTS

spot pointed out to us. We need to remember that what doesn't feel comfortable in the moment can be for our own good.

important being to glorify God in all that they do, in whatever direction He chooses to lead them.

The Marathon of Life
Life with Christ is a marathon with hurdles, hills and valleys along the way. Each challenge is uniquely situated to help us grow in our walk with Christ.

Good Investments
Someday, we will be called to account for how we have handled our wealth, our influence and our time—our lives. The question will be, What kind of stewards have we been?

Worldview War
There is a constant struggle between the Christian and humanistic worldviews. As such, we need to have a sense of situational awareness—we need to know our worldview, and then enter into the arena.

No One Sees
There are many times in life when we think that no one is watching and we can "adjust" our lie in life, tweaking the facts, thinking we will get away with it. But that is not living a life of integrity.

A Sovereign God
A belief in a sovereign God shapes our values, morals, business decisions, educational priorities and laws of the land. Without a sovereign God, a survival of the fittest, smartest or wittiest could prevail.

A Stand
There is power in the ability to formulate an idea and take a stand. A good disagreement helps formulate great ideas and leave merely good ones by the wayside.

A Simple Act

Some Christians get trapped in the mind-set that unless they are doing something overly spiritual, they are somehow spiritually immature. Yet we can make our life one of devotion wherever we are simply by living a life pleasing to Christ.

Character and Destiny

We must not try to avoid the hard times—God has placed them in our life for a reason. When we embrace adversity, our character rises to the level necessary to meet our destiny.

Winning the 1,500 meters at the 1972 Olympic Trials in Eugene, Oregon. Of all the races I have run, the most important race is the one I live each day for Christ.

INTRODUCTION

The great missionary Adoniram Judson once wrote, "A life once spent is irrevocable. It remains to be contemplated throughout eternity." I want to live a life worth contemplating throughout eternity, so that on my final day I can rest content in knowing I fulfilled the purpose of my design. This life is made up of one day built on another day, built on another. Each day brings us one step closer to eternity. None of us is given an unlimited number of days upon this Earth.

It's hard to believe that I'm nearly 60 years old now. It was just yesterday that I was striding down the backstretch in pursuit of world records and Olympic medals, and yet the mirror tells me that those days are nearly 40 years in the past. We must use the time given us wisely and consider each day as an opportunity to grow in our walk with Christ.

We must never allow our pursuit of becoming more Christlike to stagnate. When lived to its fullest, the life with Christ is a dynamic one of challenges, of dying to self, of being stretched, of rejoicing, of even weeping in the midst of the trials. It's my hope that as you read this book, you will see life as a great adventure and, as the writer of Hebrews 12 so wonderfully writes, a race with Christ.

We've each been given a great gift by God—our individual lives. Each life is of inestimable worth, and we are called to run the race of life with courage, keeping our eyes on Jesus. Christ calls us forward. As the characters in *The Last Battle* by C.S. Lewis say, "Further up and further in."

I hope that this book will be an encouragement to you to go higher up and higher in with your walk with Christ. Each chapter is a life-lesson that I've learned or a story that has inspired me. At the end of each chapter are questions that I hope will give you food for thought. There are also Scriptures listed that I would encourage you to read to help give each chapter deeper meaning.

None of us is in the place where we have reached perfection, and we never will be in this life. But I hope in some small way this book will provide mile markers along the way for you to encourage you as you run your race with Christ.

In the end, I hope you and I can both say, "I have truly lived a life worth contemplating."

Congressman Jim Ryun
Washington, D.C.
June, 2006

THE COURAGE TO RUN

INSPIRATION FOR

WINNING THE RACE

OF YOUR LIFE

THE RACE

It was a warm June night in 1965, and thousands of sports fans filled Balboa Stadium in San Diego, California. As I toed the line of the nationally televised mile final at the AAU championships, I glanced at my fellow competitors. We were an elite group of some of the fastest milers in the world. Many eyes were on Peter Snell, the young man who had dominated the Olympics the previous summer, winning two gold medals. With his muscular physique, he was intimidating, especially to a tall, skinny 18-year-old runner from Kansas (me).

In the weeks preceding the AAU National Championships, I had competed against Snell three times and lost each time. But I was gaining ground. In the race before the AAU championships, I had finished within a second of him.

The plan that night in San Diego was simple: I was to shadow Snell until the last 300 meters and then take the lead. Once in front, I was to ratchet up the pace until it was a flat-out sprint for the finish line. I knew I had done the training. My recent workouts proved I was as strong and as fit as I had ever been. Now it was time to muster up the courage to run.

I had a plan, but as we ran, I had to adjust. For most of the race, I stayed near the middle of the pack. Then, as we entered the backstretch on the last lap, I bolted into the lead. The crowd roared its approval. The

American record holder in the mile, Jim Grelle, appeared on my right shoulder, running hard. I held him off. As we sped around the curve, Snell surged past Grelle. Gritting my teeth, I dug deeper, legs and lungs burning. Down the homestretch Snell and I battled every inch of the way to the finish line. I won by the narrowest of margins. Through the pain of lactic acid, I heard the time announced: 3:55.3—a new American record for the mile.

Off the track, each of us also runs a race—the race of life.

Let us lay aside every weight, and the sin that so easily ensnares us, and let us run with endurance the race that is set before us, looking unto Jesus, the author and finisher of our faith (Hebrews 12:1-2).

To successfully run any race (on the track or in life), we must make decisions both in preparation and during competition. In San Diego, I had to decide how to best compete against some of the world's fastest runners, and then adapt along the way. This required my body and mind to work together. The race of life works much the same way.

I believe that faith is a combination of the head, heart and soul. The head part involves right choices. Just as I trained to become the best miler in the world, so we as Christians must train ourselves spiritually to become more like Christ. In our lives, we must decide to lay aside sin, focus on Christ, and love and serve Him with our mind, heart and soul.

What decisions are you making today that will draw you closer to Christ? What kind of time are you taking to become spiritually fit as you run the race of life?

⌇

Today's reading: Hebrews 12:1-2

⌇

SMALL THINGS DONE WELL

In the days leading up to the Olympic trials in the summer of 1964, my coach, Bob Timmons, and I knew I was one of the top milers in America, even though I was only 17 and a junior in high school. I was within striking distance of being one of the top three U.S. runners, a designation that would send me to the Olympics in Tokyo. To find a way to run my fastest, I trained hard.

Because of the intense summer heat in Kansas, I did my long runs early in the morning. Oftentimes I would wait until 8 or 9 o'clock at night to run my track workouts. Since I was spending the summer in Lawrence, I trained at Memorial Stadium on the University of Kansas campus, using car headlights to light the track at night.

Coach Timmons was known for sometimes assigning quarter-mile runs (one lap) up to 40 times in one night—that's 10 miles! By the end of the workout, I was always exhausted, drenched in sweat, and ready to go to sleep. One night, after training particularly hard, I finished my last repetition and was eager to warm-down when Timmie opened the gate at the end of Memorial Stadium. He called me over and pointed up the Campanile Hill, which starts right outside the stadium, and told me to start running repeats of it. It is roughly 250 yards up to the top. I didn't want to scale the hill that night, but I had no choice. I staggered up, then back to the bottom, then up and down again until Timmie said, "Enough."

Weeks later, in the finals of the Olympic trials, I was in fifth place coming into the final homestretch. I was tired, but so was everyone else. Somehow I found more strength. I crept into fourth place, and then with 20 meters to go, I pulled even for third. It was a footrace to the finish. With 10 meters to go, I edged ahead for the final spot on the 1964 Olympic team. The photo finish revealed that I had beaten Jim Grelle by about a foot.

Proverbs 22:29 reads: "Do you see a man who excels in his work? He will stand before kings; He will not stand before unknown men." This proverb applies to everyone who seeks greatness; to excel in our work, we must do the small things well because it is in doing the small things well that we achieve greater things.

I went on to become a world record holder in the mile, 1,500 meters and the half-mile, and made another two Olympic teams. But success did not happen by chance, it did not occur overnight, nor did it come without God giving me the talent. Success came by doing one small thing well, and then another, and then another. Now, many years and many small things done well later, by God's grace, I have achieved much in my life that I would never have dreamed possible. I am convinced that as Christians we should seek to do everything well (small and big) as unto the Lord. And we need to keep doing them well until God says, "Enough." In doing things well, opportunities will present themselves that we never thought possible.

What small thing do you need to do well today? What three small things do you need to do well this week?

✑

Today's reading: Proverbs 22:29; Colossians 3:23

✑

JUSTICE AND MERCY

In Shakespeare's *The Merchant of Venice*, Bassanio needs money in order to woo Lady Portia. Shylock agrees to loan Bassanio 3,000 ducats if Bassanio's friend Antonio will put up his property as the bond. Shylock hates Antonio and asks for a pound of flesh if Antonio cannot pay the debt. Antonio agrees to the deal, but his ships are lost at sea, and he finds himself unable to pay the loan. Shylock is intent upon taking Antonio's heart as the pound of flesh, and while the court is trying to decide Antonio's fate, Lady Portia enters the courtroom, dressed in disguise as a lawyer. She looks at Shylock and tells him he must have mercy upon Antonio. When Shylock demands to know why he must be merciful, Portia replies:

> The quality of mercy is not strain'd;
> It droppeth as the gentle rain from heaven
> Upon the place beneath: it is twice bless'd;
> It blesseth him that gives and him that takes:
> 'Tis mightiest in the mightiest, it becomes
> The throned monarch better than his crown,
> His scepter shows the force of temporal power,
> The attribute to awe and majesty,
> Wherein doth sit the dread and fear of kings,

It is an attribute to God himself;
And earthly power doth then show likest God's
When mercy seasons justice.[1]

We see the same themes of mercy and justice running thru Matthew 18:21-35. The king demonstrates mercy by forgiving the servant's debt. We also see, however, the servant, who had just been forgiven, not showing mercy to another person, but insisting on justice instead. As a result, the unforgiving servant is brought once more before the king and shown what happens when there is no mercy, only justice.

Those of us who have accepted Christ can consider the great mercy that has been shown to us. We were lost, and in our humanness, we could never have experienced forgiveness for our sins or hoped for eternal life. In God's tender, loving mercy, He sent His only Son to die for us to pay the debt we owe because of our sins—a debt He did not owe and one that we could never pay. Because of Christ's death, we can know forgiveness and eternal life. In light of such mercy shown to us, can we not show mercy and forgiveness to others?

Family members and work associates will offend us. Our claims of wrongdoing may be just, but in the balance of eternity, what can ever compare to God's mercy toward us? Nothing. In the light of such mercy shown to us, can we not show mercy to those around us? Gestures of mercy are not easy to make. In some lives there have been great tragedies. But the magnitude of the mercy and love shown to us compels us to be merciful, and it is in the process of being merciful that we can become more like Christ.

Think of someone who has wronged you. How can you show him or her mercy today?

*

Today's reading: Matthew 18:23-35; Colossians 3:12-13

*

THE WONDER OF IT ALL

Like many Americans in the 1950s, my father was intrigued by the space race between the United States and Russia. I still remember very clearly the day the news broke that the Russians had launched into space a satellite called "Sputnik." Although I was very young at the time, I could feel the angst that filled the Kansas countryside and the entire nation. The Russians appeared to be holding the upper hand in space, and we didn't really know what it all meant or where it would all lead.

My father worked the late shift at the Boeing plant in Wichita, Kansas. When he came home from work, he always searched the early morning skies, trying to find Sputnik as it hurtled through space.

Several times he woke me up to search the skies with him. The first morning I saw Sputnik, I was awestruck. The satellite was an 85-pound object, hundreds of miles away, circling the earth, and I, a little boy, could see it. On those early mornings, standing with my father and watching the heavens, I would wonder, "Who is God? How big is He?" I thought God had to be pretty big seeing as there were so many stars and planets.

Psalm 19 paints a picture of the heavens declaring the glory of God and of the firmament showing His handiwork. Genesis 1 proclaims that He made the sun, moon and stars and placed them in the heavens to give light to our planet. It's not hard to imagine God, like a master artisan, creating the stars in His hands, giving each a name, and then placing each one on the vast canvas of the heavens.

I look about me at this world and I see the tender care of God, His personal touch in even the tiniest of details. I see Him in the intricate beauty of a butterfly, the vibrant colors of a rainbow, the strength and majesty of a redwood. I see Him in a delicate snowflake, a springtime bloom of the Eastern Redbud. I hear Him in laughter and joy, even in sorrow and tears. And then, like the psalmist David, I lift my eyes up from this Earth and consider the heavens, the moon and the stars.

Even though I am much older now than I was on those mornings when I stood with my father looking for Sputnik, the majesty and splendor of the night skies still amaze me. Indeed, on a clear, crisp night in Kansas, it seems as if heaven is filled with a million stars. The vastness of my Heavenly Father's creation amazes me, and then I consider that He who made this universe also made me. He cared for us, loved us before we even knew Him, and sent His Son to die for us so that we might have eternal life—the wonder of it all.

What do you see when you gaze up at the sky ablaze with all of the stars of the universe? What amazes you most about a God so big and so personal that He knew you before you were born?

⌒♪⌒

Today's reading: Psalms 8:3-5 and 19:1-2

⌒♪⌒

A REASONABLE FAITH

"Belief," "trust," "confidence"—the *Oxford English Dictionary* includes these three words in its definition of "faith." We encounter these three words and actions each day of our lives. Because of this, I believe the word "faith" comes to life in real, everyday events.

I've always liked to think the writer of Hebrews felt the same way. In Hebrews 11, a working definition of faith appears that clearly has something to do with things of substance. Within this understanding appear cognitive and relational components. Evidently the men and women in chapter 11 had a reason to have the faith in God that they did, a faith that was not simply an emotional response to a belief system. It's as if the writer of Hebrews is saying, "Look at Abraham. He believed God. Did God let him down? And look there at Moses? See how God guided him?"

The writer shows his readers example after example of a reasonable faith. There is a pattern to it all, both in the technique and the actual events themselves. Sarah, though old, gave birth to Isaac "because she judged Him [God] faithful who had promised" (Hebrews 11:11). By faith, the people of Israel brought down the walls of Jericho. Therefore, it stands to reason that this faith of which the writer speaks is a rational one. It is a decision made to put trust in God because He has proven Himself trustworthy and a fulfiller of His promises again and again.

I think that too often we become imbued with the ideas of Danish philosopher Søren Keirkegaard, who separated reason and faith, suggesting that when it came to human beings, the two could not function in the same realm of thought. The upper level of Kierkegaardism includes faith, or nonreason. In the lower level resides pessimism, or reason. Reason, Kierkegaard concludes, leads to despair, so humans must find a release and throw themselves into nonreason, or faith.

I know this simplifies Kierkegaard, but still the question arises: What kind of faith would require its followers to divorce themselves from reason and blindly launch into the unknown without any assurance of what lies ahead? There is no substance (or biblical foundation) to that kind of faith. I firmly believe God gave us minds for a purpose and within each of us the ability to reason. A. W. Tozer said it best: "Faith creates nothing; it simply reckons upon that which is already there."[1] For me, that is faith. It simply reckons on that which has already been revealed to us. The readers of Hebrews, past and present, do not have to launch themselves into a blind faith. They know of God's existence, and they know that He will never leave or forsake His own; this has been made evident again and again throughout history.

What kind of faith do we have? Is it a wishful faith, a hope that there might be someone or something greater than us out there somewhere? Or is it a reasonable faith, one that looks at the world around us, sees the hand of God and says, "I believe"?

What kind of faith do you have? What reasons has God given you to believe? What actions has He taken to assure you that He will never forsake you?

⤠

Today's reading: Hebrews 11:1-6,30-39

⤠

COLONIES OF HEAVEN

In 1630, the newly elected governor of the Massachusetts Bay Colony, John Winthrop, and 700 fellow Puritans set sail for the New World. Fleeing the persecution of King Charles I and the Anglican Church, Winthrop and company were hoping to create in America a Christian community that would be an example to the rest of the world. The popular telling of the story features an incident that occurred on the deck of the *Arabella*, one of the Massachusetts Bay Company's ships. As governor-cum-preacher, Winthrop delivered a sermon titled, "Model of Christian Charity." He reminded everyone on board why they were going to this new England.

> The Lord will be our God, and delight to dwell among us, as His own people, and will command a blessing upon us in all our ways, so that we shall see much more of His wisdom, power, goodness, and truth, than formerly we have been acquainted with. We shall find that the God of Israel is among us, when ten of us shall be able to resist a thousand of our enemies; when He shall make us a praise and glory that men shall say of succeeding plantations, 'may the Lord make it like that of New England.' For we must consider that we shall be as a city set on a hill. The eyes of all people are upon us.

Just like these Puritans, today we too must consider ourselves as "colonies of heaven," placed in our specific spheres of influence for a reason. As Christians we should ask ourselves, "What can we do in our community to be a light for Christ?" and "Am I demonstrating what it means to live the Christian life?" The truth is, once people find out we follow Christ, they will closely watch to see if what we confess with our mouths lines up with how we actually live.

Second Corinthians 5:20 reads,

> We are ambassadors for Christ, as though God were pleading through us: we implore you on Christ's behalf, be reconciled to God.

We should see ourselves as ambassadors for Christ. Ambassadors are sent to represent their nation in a foreign land, both in word and in action. Many times they are the only personal representative that others in the foreign land will see, and relationships between nations can potentially be nurtured or damaged by an ambassador.

Sometimes we might be the only Christian with whom those around us will interact. Do they see Christ? Do they see "colonies of heaven" when they see us? I always tell my children that we as Christians are the fifth Gospel. To be that fifth Gospel—and to be ambassadors for Christ—we should, in the words of St. Francis of Assisi, "Preach Christ at all times; if necessary, use words."

How can you be an ambassador for Christ today? When an unbeliever looks at you, does he or she see a colony of heaven?

∞

Today's reading: 2 Corinthians 5:20-21

∞

ONE EYE ON ETERNITY

It has often been said that men and women who truly do great things in this life have kept one eye on eternity. When I consider the lives of committed Christians such as William Wilberforce; Lord Ashley Cooper, Seventh Earl of Shaftesbury; John Wesley; John Newton; Theodore Weld; Angelina Grimke; C. T. Studd, and others, I see a common thread. To a person, their focus was on Christ and eternity while fulfilling their time on Earth.

Some historians contend that William Wilberforce could have been prime minister of England if he had not committed his political career to seeing slavery abolished. Lord Shaftesbury used his wealth and political career in an endless battle to prevent the exploitation of women and children in England's mines and factories. Angelina Grimke left behind the life of a rich slaveholding family in South Carolina to become one of the first great abolitionists in America. C. T. Studd gave up a successful athletic career and large inheritance to become a missionary. Each of these people were counted fools at one time or another, but they were willing to lay down this world's fame and wealth to achieve truly great things. *They had one eye on eternity.*

I earnestly desire this same kind of eternal perspective. All the world can offer—fame, fortune and power—if obtained only for one's self, are mirages in the light of eternity. Matthew asks, "What is a man profited if he gains the whole world, and loses his own soul? Or what will a man give in exchange for his soul?" (16:26). The question is not answered directly; rather it is implied: nothing. All the world's temporal gain can never compare with the eternal reward of heaven.

Consider this world. A finite point in infinite space is a speck in time; that is what this world, from its beginning to end, is in the span of eternity. I would take eternity over a speck anytime.

I have heard the cheers of thousands of people as I drove toward the finish line to break another world record. I have stood in front of thousands of television cameras, and I have been on the cover of *Sports Illustrated*, *Newsweek* and *Track and Field* numerous times. But the glory and fame of this world is as dust compared with Christ.

I am reminded of the hymn, "I'd Rather Have Jesus." The second stanza goes like this:

I'd rather have Jesus than men's applause
I'd rather be faithful to His dear cause
I'd rather have Jesus than worldwide fame
I'd rather be true to His holy name.

I know from personal experience that the applause of men fades away, but that's all right. The applause I never want to hear end is God's applause. Someday when I pass into eternity, I want to hear Him say, "Well done, good and faithful servant" (Matt. 25:23).

I want to use the talents that God has given me to live for Him. What talents do you have that can be used for His glory? What do you need to change today for that to happen?

∽

Today's reading: Matthew 6:19-21 and 16:24-27

∽

TOUGH DECISIONS

I have been a member of the U.S. House of Representatives for 10 years. During this time I have cast thousands of votes on thousands of measures. Most of the decisions made by Congress never make the news and remain largely unknown to the average citizen. Nonetheless, I take each vote seriously, and a few of the decisions I have made have stuck with me because they were challenging votes—specifically the bankruptcy measure in 2002 and the Medicare bill in 2003.

In both cases, I found myself battling the leadership in my party and the White House. The bankruptcy bill had an amendment attached that would have severely discouraged peaceful protests at abortion clinics. I knew we needed bankruptcy reform, but I informed leadership that while that amendment was attached, I would not be voting for the bill. The "whipping" of the vote and the arm-twisting involved became intense, but thankfully the bankruptcy bill was defeated. (I later voted in favor of a revised version that did not include the abortion clinic protest amendment.)

The Medicare reform bill was nothing more than a new multibillion dollar entitlement plan. Along with 24 other conservatives, I refused to support it. The vote was extremely close, and the White House desperately wanted it to pass. I remember sitting on the House floor with a member of Republican leadership standing over me: "Jim, we need this vote."

The president even called and asked me to change my vote. To both men, I respectfully said no. For me, it was difficult to stand my ground and stick with my principles. It would have been much easier to capitulate to leadership and to White House demands.

Making tough decisions and being guided by principle reminds me of William Wilberforce, the great British abolitionist. In 1789, as a young member of the House of Commons, Wilberforce began his epic battle against slavery. One day, he stood before the House of Commons and spoke for three hours against the slave trade. He concluded with these words: "Policy . . . is not my principle, and I am not ashamed to say it. There is a principle above every thing that is political; and when I reflect on the command which says, 'Thou shalt do no murder,' believing the authority to be divine, how can I dare set up my reasonings of my own against it. And when we think of eternity, and of the future consequences of all human conduct, what is there in this life that should make any man contradict the dictates of his conscience, the principle of justice, and the laws of religion, and of God?"[1]

Wilberforce's battle against slavery, of far greater importance than a vote on Medicare or bankruptcy, was unpopular at first. He spent the last 24 years of his life working for the end of slavery in the British Emprire. Finally, when Wilberforce was on his deathbed, the emancipation of slaves took place.

Wilberforce reminds me that in my career as a congressman, principle comes first, not political pragmatism. Each one of us, regardless of where we are in life, must decide what principles will guide us, and then no matter what the temptations or pressures, we must stick to them.

What principles guide your life? How will these principles affect the decisions you make today?

∽

Today's reading: Luke 12:4-5; Hebrews 13:5-6

∽

INTEGRITY

On August 2, 1776, 56 men signed their names to the Declaration of Independence.[1] With one stroke of a pen they pledged their lives, fortunes and sacred honor for the sake of American liberty. Some years later, Benjamin Rush told John Adams how many of the men thought signing the Declaration was like signing their own death warrants.

Rush recounted how Colonel Benjamin Harrison of Virginia, a giant of a man, and Elbridge Gerry, a frail delegate from Massachusetts, approached the table to sign the document. Harrison looked at Gerry and said, "I shall have a distinct advantage over you, Mr. Gerry, when we are all hung for what we are doing. From the size and weight of my body I shall die in a few minutes, but from the lightness of your body, you will dance in the air an hour or two before you are dead!"[2]

Another signer was Abraham Clark. Clark had two sons. Both eventually served in the Continental Army during the Revolutionary War, were captured by the British and were thrown onto the prison ship *Jersey*. Although it is not well known, during the Revolutionary War, more American soldiers died on the British prison ships than on the field of battle. Of the 16 prison ships anchored in New York harbor, the *Jersey* was the worst. So many American prisoners died from disease and starvation on board the *Jersey* that every morning the British jailers would open the hatches and yell down, "Rebels, turn out your dead!"

The British realized who the Clark sons were and threw the eldest into solitary confinement, with no food, only water. For a while, other prisoners forced food through the keyhole and kept the son alive. The British contacted Abraham Clark, who was well aware of where his sons were, and made an offer to him. If he removed his name from the Declaration of Independence, his sons would go free.

I have no doubt that Abraham Clark wrestled with the offer—any father would when faced with the choice of having his two sons set free from what could be their deaths. But Abraham sent the British back a simple message: "No." Through a series of events and prisoner exchanges, Clark's sons were eventually set free, but I am struck by Abraham Clark's decision. He pledged his life, his fortune and his sacred honor when he signed the Declaration, and even when faced with a very difficult choice, remained true to his word.

> LORD, who may dwell in Your sanctuary? Who may live on your holy hill? . . . He who keeps his [word] even when it hurts (Psalm 15:1,4, *NIV*).

Abraham Clark kept his word, even when it hurt. We as Christians, though not likely to face as hard a decision as Clark, still face difficult choices. Big or little, we must realize that as Christians, when we accepted Christ, we pledged to follow Christ's commands. As such, we must always show integrity between what we have confessed in accepting Christ and how we live our lives.

What is the biggest decision you will have to make today? How will you maintain your integrity when making that choice?

❧

Today's reading: Psalm 15:1-4

❧

FOR HIS GLORY

People often think that my running career brought me a great deal of financial gain. Sorry to say, it did not. Strict amateur track and field regulations forced me to return many prizes I won, including watches, television sets and typewriters. I couldn't even take home money for speaking engagements. The six-figure appearance fees that top runners command today were unheard of at the time. Once I turned pro, I did make good money and hung up my spikes with some savings in the bank—but I was by no means wealthy.

When I retired from track and field, my fourth child, Catharine, had just been born. I earned my living as a photojournalist, so money was tight. My wife, Anne, and I had committed our lives to Christ several years earlier, and we made our home in Lawrence, Kansas. It was such a struggle to make ends meet that I clearly remember a group of young Christians who would deliver groceries to our doorstep almost every day for a period of time. They always delivered broccoli, and I remember having broccoli for lunch and dinner in myriad ways: broccoli with butter, broccoli soup, steamed broccoli—anyway you can imagine broccoli being served, we did.

One morning during this time, I was reading my Bible and praying with Anne. We read Luke 18—the wonderful passage that recounts the time Jesus told the rich young ruler to give away all he had so that he could follow Him. The young man walked away in sorrow because he was very wealthy and did not want to give up what he owned.

As Anne and I prayed that morning, we both felt strongly that we were to give away our last $100 to our local Episcopal church. My initial reaction was something like this: "Lord, that's my last $100 right now, and we're having a tough time making ends meet!" I admit, I was anxious. Nonetheless, Anne and I couldn't shake the conviction, so we quickly wrote out a check and sent it off before our doubts overcame our faith.

I have never regretted the decision, and we were never in want. Scripture assures us, "I [David] have never seen the righteous forsaken, or their seed out begging for bread" (Psalm 37:25).

Some people think that once they have tithed, they do not need to talk with God about the rest of their finances. Not so. We gave away the little money we had at the time, but it was God's anyway. It was a simple decision to make because all that we have is His and should be used for His glory. To this day Anne and I make a practice of giving as God directs us to give, and we have taught our children to do the same. I truly believe that everything we possess—talent, money, time, influence, and even broccoli—is God's. It takes spiritual courage, but we must ask ourselves constantly, "How can I use what has been given to me for His glory?"

What talents, time, possessions and influence has God given to you? What is He asking you to give away today—for His glory?

⁂

Today's reading: Psalm 37:25; Luke 18:18-23

⁂

My coach my senior year in high school, J. D. Edminston, informs me after the finish of the 1965 A.A.U. Championships that not only have I beaten Peter Snell, but that as an 18-year-old, I'd just set the American record in the mile at 3:55.3. That time would stand as the high school mile record until 2001.

As a 17-year-old junior in high school, training for the 1964 Olympic Trials. I would make the team in the 1,500 meters, and this photo (above right) would make the cover of *Sports Illustrated*. Juggling my studies (above left) and running 100 miles a week was never easy, but somehow I managed to break a few world records and graduate from the University of Kansas with a degree in photo journalism.

The beginning of the 1965 A.A.U. Championships. As an 18-year-old recent graduate of high school, I was facing Peter Snell, the gold medalist in both the 1,500 and 800 meters in the 1964 Olympics, Josef Odlozil, silver medalist in the 1964 1,500 meters, and Jim Grelle, U.S. Olympian and American record holder in the mile. At the start, I had every intention of winning the race.

The finish of the 1965 A.A.U. Championships. My race plan worked to perfection, and down the homestretch, it was a matter of finding the courage to fight through the pain. I held off Peter Snell by the slimmest of margins and set the new American record in the mile of 3:55.3.

PERSEVERANCE

Aesop tells the story of the tortoise and hare. The hare made fun of the tortoise. "What a slow way you have!" he said. "How you creep along!"

"Do I?" said the tortoise. "Try and race with me and I'll beat you."

"What a boaster you are," said the hare. "But come! I will race with you. Whom shall we ask to mark off the finish line and see that the race is fair?"

"Let us try the fox," said the tortoise.

The fox showed them where they were to start, and how far they were to run, and then he sent them off. The tortoise lost no time. He jogged straight on. The hare leaped along swiftly for a few minutes until he had left the tortoise far behind. He knew he could reach the mark very quickly, so he lay down by the road under a shady tree and took a nap. By and by he awoke and remembered the race. He sprang up and ran as fast as he could. But when he reached the finish mark, the tortoise was already there!

"Slow and steady wins the race," said the fox.

I've always found it fascinating how true that fable is in real life. Calvin Coolidge once wrote:

Nothing in this world can take the place of persistence. Talent will not; nothing is more common than unsuccessful men with talent.

Genius will not; unrewarded genius is almost a proverb. Education will not; the world is full of educated derelicts. Persistence and determination alone are omnipotent.

Many times I have seen the virtue of perseverance triumph over undisciplined ability. God gave me great talent as a runner, but I never considered myself the most gifted runner. I often told my sons that some of the competitors I raced had greater ability than me, yet due to circumstances, they quit before their running truly blossomed. I continued on, my dreams driving me to succeed. Those dreams gave me the determination to persevere through the tough times. One day, after so much hard work, things began to fall into place. I suddenly began to run times that astounded both my coach and me. The rest is history, I suppose, but the lesson remains not only from my life, but also from the tortoise. Hard, steady, persistent work pays off.

There are many qualities linked to perseverance. Hard work goes hand in hand with hope, which gives us the ability to believe that there is something better beyond the present. Hope stirs up within us the strength to persevere through the tough times, when all seems to be going wrong. Even in nature, we see that after the rain the sun shines and the flowers bloom. It's after the darkest hour of the night that morning comes. Many times, before we can achieve something truly great, we must first endure pain. Before we can truly find peace and victory, we must sweat and work hard.

Those who walk with Christ are people "who by patient continuance in doing good seek for glory, honor, and immortality" (Romans 2:7). That's us.

Think of a goal that seems too difficult to reach. Ask yourself, do you have the hope to go steady, work hard and persevere? Are you going to be a hare or a tortoise?

☙

Today's reading: Romans 2:7

☙

HIS PLEASURE

In the movie *Chariots of Fire*, Eric Liddell struggles with his call to the mission field in China. In one scene, he looks at his sister and says, "Jenny, I know God made me for a purpose, but He also made me fast, and when I run, I feel His pleasure."[1] Eric delayed going to China in order to train for the 1924 Olympics, at which he won the gold medal in the 400 meters competition, setting a world record in the process.

The next year while in his running prime, he put athletics aside to go on the mission field. Eric was such a hero in his native Scotland that when he was leaving Edinburgh, thousands of people showed up at the train station to see him off. As the train began slowly rolling away, Liddell threw down the train window, leaned out, and began leading the crowd in the hymn "Jesus Shall Reign."

> *Jesus shall reign where're the sun*
> *Doth its successive journeys run;*
> *His kingdom spread from shore to shore*
> *'Til moon shall wax and wane no more.*

Here was a young man who in the world's eyes had everything. Yet he left his worldly success behind to pursue what he knew to be even greater glory.

Eric served in China for nearly 20 years, his international running career over, but still running in various races when he could. Athletes he raced against said he could have won gold again in 1928, and, if he had chosen, become the greatest 800 meters runner of his time. Instead he worked diligently in the mission field. But when the Japanese invaded China, they placed Liddell and foreign missionaries in an internment camp. Several years later, while in the internment camp, and only in his 40s, Eric died of a brain tumor.

Some people might argue that Eric wasted his life: A young man in his prime goes to the far ends of the world and dies a prisoner in a war that did not involve him. Nothing could be further from the truth. Eric's life was based on running a race all right—a race with Christ. He knew God had made him fast, and he ran for his Master's glory. Once Eric had won Olympic gold, he knew there was a greater race to be run, one that would take him further than any Olympic competition.

I don't know if Eric Liddell ever really said, "When I run I feel His pleasure," or if that phrase was a Hollywood screenwriter's creation. But it is a true statement. When we are in God's will, fulfilling the purposes for which we were designed, we feel God's pleasure. Our race may not be in a stadium or before crowds. It might be in China or some far-off place as it was for Eric. It might be in the U.S. Congress, as it now is for me. Or it might be in the marketplace, at home, at school or in a church.

What race has Christ given you to run? Do you feel His pleasure?

✧

Today's reading: 1 Corinthians 9:24-27

✧

TRUE CONFIDENCE

Coach Timmons knew how to coach. He devised all sorts of workouts for me, many with specific purposes. The confidence workouts did exactly as the name implied—they built up my confidence. One workout was a 10-mile run—I had to finish in 52 minutes.

This may get a little technical if you are not a runner, but follow me for a moment. I was what is called a middle-distance runner and I had 46 second speed when running 400 meters. I strongly disliked running anything further than 3 miles, but I knew that if I could complete the confidence workout, my endurance would improve. Just a little bit more track and field stats to make my point: I would sometimes run 400 meters in 60 seconds 20 consecutive times, with 60 seconds rest between each repetition, which would demonstrate that my speed endurance was where it should be. Sometimes before a big race, Timmie would give me an even more intense workout. Every repetition, no matter the distance, would raise my confidence as a runner.

On a much deeper and more important level, our confidence in life should come through Christ, not education, not talent or intelligence, but from the Giver and Creator of our intelligence and talents.

I was given a gift to run. For a time, I had a mistaken view of it, and I found my confidence and identity in running. But when I went through a period of bad races (yes, even Olympians have bad races), it became very clear that running was a poor source for true confidence. When I came to know Christ as my Savior, my entire perspective on life changed. My source of confidence no longer was in my physical talents; rather, it was in Christ. When I was elected to Congress, my confidence could have shifted to my ability to win elections, lead people and legislate in Washington, D.C. Thankfully, it did not. To this day, my confidence and my identity flow from my relationship with Christ.

I remind myself of what Christ has done for me and that He considers me of great importance. The very Son of God suffered on the cross because He loves us. His shed blood has forgiven our sins and this free gift is open to each of us.

With joy and singing, God dances over us. Think about that for a moment–the Creator of heaven and Earth dances over us. The Old Testament book of Jeremiah reminds us that He loves us with an everlasting love (see 31:3), and the Gospel of John tells us that God so loved the world that He gave up, of His own volition, His only Son so that we can know eternal life (see John 3:14-16). Because of the love and the joy that God has for each one of us who are His children, and because we know that each one of us is unique and made by Him for a purpose, we can have the confidence to live a life that is pleasing to Him.

Picture God dancing over you. How does that make you feel? What does that do for your confidence in the destiny for which you have been created?

✑

Today's reading: Jeremiah 31:3; Zephaniah 3:17; John 3:14-16

✑

GOD IS

My wife and I loved reading C. S. Lewis to our children. Who doesn't? We were pleased to see *The Lion, the Witch and the Wardrobe* finally make it to the big screen in 2005, and we hope there are more to come. We can all learn from the Penvensie children.

Remember when Lucy quizzed Mr. and Mrs. Beaver about Aslan? "Is . . . is he a man?" she asked.

"Aslan a man!" said Mr. Beaver sternly. "Certainly not. I tell you he is the King of the wood and the son of the great Emperor-Beyond-the-Sea. Don't you know who is the King of the Beasts? Aslan is a lion—the Lion, the great Lion."

Mrs. Beaver added, "That you will, my dearie, and make no mistake, if there's anyone who can appear before Aslan without their knees knocking, they're either braver than most or else just silly."

"Then he isn't safe?" asked Lucy.

"Safe?" said Mr. Beaver. "Don't you hear what Mrs. Beaver tells you? Who said anything about being safe? 'Course he isn't safe. But he's good. He's the King, I tell you."[1]

We can ask the same question about God: Who is He? It is a fair question. Of course, we know that God's son, Jesus, is the King. And God Himself is good. But there's more. My wife and I always taught our children that God IS. By this we mean that He is always present, always watching. He is love and He is just. There is a proper fear and respect that must be rendered toward Him. We always taught our children that God loves them, created them for His glory and has a purpose for each one. But we also taught them that God holds the power of eternity in His hands. The righteous fear of God begins with the realization of who He is. Such wisdom gives a man or woman enough courage to stay on the right path, particularly when temptation comes along.

My son Ned was working in the fishing business in Alaska the summer of 1994. He and two of the fishermen he worked with were shooting the breeze at the end of the day, and one of the fishermen pulled out some marijuana. He asked Ned if he wanted to join the others as they smoked the joint. My son laughed as he told me the story. The fishermen had tempted him with the joint and prodded him, saying, "Your parents aren't here, and your brother isn't here. No one will ever know." My son simply replied, "But God sees me."

Psalm 139 speaks of God always being with us. God is. He is omniscient. He is omnipresent. There is nowhere we can go where He is not with us. Although others might not see our actions, He does—even in our private moments. If we have a tendency to cave in to temptation, God's seeing our every move might intimidate us. On the other hand, if we attempt to rebuff temptation, we can have peace of mind knowing that God sees how we seek to respect Him, even in our private moments.

Do you find fear or comfort in knowing that God sees you right now? How will you respond to temptation today, knowing that God is there with you?

❦

Today's reading: Job 28:20-28; Psalm 139:1-12; Matthew 10:27-31

❦

DUTY

John Quincy Adams had been in the political arena since he was 11. A secretary to the American ambassador in the court of Queen Anne of Russia, Adams had gone on to be an ambassador, a U.S. representative, a senator and then president. In 1828, Adams sought to be re-elected as president, but lost to Andrew Jackson. In defeat, Adams presumed that his years of public service were done. He was 61 years old, so retirement would be understandable.

However, the people of Massachusetts's Twelfth District wanted Adams to represent them in the U.S. House of Representatives. So Adams, somewhat reluctantly, agreed to do what no other president has ever done: At the end of his term as president, he left the White House and in 1831 he became a congressman. Slavery was a huge issue at the time. Congress had outlawed the importation of slaves in 1808, but it was still practiced, particularly in the Southern states. In the 1830s, there were more than one million slaves in America, and Adams was determined to end slavery. The battle was a tough one, because the House was dominated by pro-slavery forces.

Every Monday, Adams brought into the House chamber hundreds of abolitionist petitions calling for the outlawing of slavery. In 1836, Southern congressmen passed a gag rule, which had the House automatically table petitions against slavery. Adams tirelessly fought the rule for eight years until finally he obtained its repeal. In 1839, he successfully defended the African slaves who overwhelmed the crew of the Spanish slave ship *Amistad*. That same year, Adams attempted to introduce amendments to the U.S. Constitution that would prevent any person born in America from being born a slave. For his unwavering efforts, Adams became known as the "Hellhound of Slavery."

One day, a newspaper reporter interviewed Adams. In the interview, the reporter asked if Adams ever grew discouraged in his battle against slavery. He looked at the reporter and simply said, "Duty is mine. The results are God's."

On the afternoon of February 21, 1848, the 80-year-old Adams was, as usual, at his desk in the House of Representatives. He was trying to rise to speak when he suddenly collapsed. He lingered on for two days before passing away. It was reported that the last words he uttered were, "This is the end of Earth. I am content."

John Quincy Adams never saw the abolition of slavery in America. But in his last term in the House, he served alongside a lanky, one-term congressman from Illinois. The one-term congressman observed Adams, was taken under his wing and was mentored by the elderly statesman. At Adams's funeral, he served as one of the pall-bearers. Thirteen years later, Abraham Lincoln was elected president and set in motion the abolition of slavery envisioned by Adams.

Adams could have retired after losing his re-election bid to Jackson. No one would have quibbled with the decision. But duty called. Duty requires consistently moving forward in the task we have been given, particularly when that assignment comes from God. And, as Adams so clearly enunciated, duty involves doing what is right and leaving the results to God.

What duty has God given you? Are you able to move forward in that assignment and leave the results to God—even if you never know the results in your lifetime?

⁂

Today's reading: Luke 4:17-19; Galatians 6:9-10

⁂

GOALS

By the spring of 1963, I had gone from being a nameless sophomore who couldn't finish workouts to one of Kansas's top high school milers. It didn't take long for both Coach Timmons and me to realize that though I had shown no proclivity toward any other sports, I was born to run.

One day on the long bus ride from Kansas City back home to Wichita, Timmie talked to me about goals. I had just sloshed my way to a 4:21 mile on a very wet cinder track at the Wyandotte High Relays.

"What do you think you can run this year?" Coach Timmons asked.

"This season?" I replied. Before he could answer, I said, "I don't know, maybe 4:15."

He nodded. "I think you can go much faster. How fast do you think you can run before you graduate?"

I thought for a minute. I knew Archie San Romani, a former Wichita East runner, held the national record at 4:08. "Maybe 4:07?" I guessed.

Out came Coach Timmons's pencil and pad, so I knew he was in earnest.

"Jim," he said, turning in his seat to look at me, "I think you can break Archie's record. In fact, I think you can be the first high school boy under 4 minutes for the mile." I was surprised. I was new to the sport of running, but I knew that only nine years earlier Roger Bannister had been the first man ever to break four minutes for the mile. I know the shock registered on my face, but Coach Timmons kept talking. It would take hard work, two workouts a day, long weekend runs of 18 and 20 miles. I wasn't fully convinced at first, but I came to the conclusion that if Coach Timmons believed I could do it, then I could.

I learned a lot of life lessons from Coach Timmons. One of the most valuable was how to set goals. He always had his runners make two sets of goals—short term (what we wanted to achieve that year) and long term (what our ultimate goal was in running as well as in life). Coach Timmons had us write down our goals so that they were in front of us at all times. That way our teammates also knew what our goals were.

Goal-setting can help in our spiritual lives, too. One of our short-term goals should to be more like Christ. Our long-term goal is heaven, and as we run down this path of life, we should echo the words of the apostle Paul, who said, "Therefore I run thus: not with uncertainty. Thus I fight: not as one who beats the air. But I discipline my body and bring it into subjection, lest, when I have preached to others, I myself should become disqualified" (1 Corinthians 9:26-27).

I encourage you to write down goals for yourself, not only for your professional career, but also for your family and for your spiritual walk. Do you want to increase your productivity at work? Set some time management goals. Do you want to be healthier? Set some physical fitness goals. Do you want to have a better quiet time in the morning? Set a goal of 15 or 20 minutes every morning of reading God's Word and turning to Him in prayer. What other goals do you have? Go ahead, write them down today.

❧

Today's reading: Proverbs 29:18

❧

THROUGH THE PAIN

In July 1966, Coach Timmons and I agreed it was time to take a crack at the mile world record. The year before I had set the American mark at 3:55.3, and earlier in the year, I had broken the world record in the half-mile and set the American record in the two mile. Several weeks before the mile world record attempt, I had run 3:53.6, one tenth of a second off Michel Jazy's world record.

The week of my record attempt, I tapered off my workouts, and by race time on Saturday, I felt rested and confident. Although Timmie and I were aiming for the world record, I made no public mention of my goal. However, before the race, I spoke with three competitors to see if they would help me with the pace through the first three laps. They readily agreed. The meet director also agreed to announce my split times over the loudspeaker at the end of each lap.

Standing at the starting line, on that hot cinder track, I was committed to breaking the world record. For several years, Coach Timmons and I had been aiming at this day, and in the few moments before the starting gun sounded, I knew that I might make history in the next four minutes. I also knew that running so fast would hold more than its fair share of pain, but that was part of competitive racing.

We passed the first 440 on world-record pace and came through the half-mile at 1:55. Everything was going as planned. Coming into the third backstretch, I felt the pace lag. Knowing that even a lapse of several strides could cost me the record, I went into the lead, even though I was 700 meters away from the finish line. I hit the three quarters of a mile mark in 2:55.3 and knew all I had to do was run the last lap in 57 seconds.

However, down the backstretch, the pace and the pain of lactic acid in my muscles began to take its toll, and with 220 yards left, I was hurting. As I came around the curve and into the final stretch, for a brief moment I thought of all the miles, all the 440s and repeat miles in practice, all the pain and the sweat I had put in just to get to this moment. I had spent years committed to breaking the record, and here was my chance.

Forcing my body through the pain, I came down the homestretch, thinking the finish line couldn't come soon enough. I broke the tape and managed to slowly walk around the curve. A few moments later, the announcement came over the loudspeaker: "In first place, Jim Ryun, 3:51.3." I had broken the world record by more than two seconds.

The apostle Paul often used the illustration of running when describing the Christian walk, and he wrote of the pursuit of a crown that will never perish, worth infinitely more than a mile world record. An athlete in pursuit of a world record must make sacrifices and keep commitments. If we are to fully pursue Christ, we must do the same.

What commitments have you made to Christ? How much pain are you willing to go through to keep those commitments?

⤐

Today's reading: James 1:4,12

⤐

RUNNING ON EMPTY

At the age of 25, I realized that something was missing in my life. According to the world's standards, I was very successful. I was the world record holder in the mile, had been on several Olympic teams, had been on the cover of *Sports Illustrated* and still had many years of running left in my legs.

Success according to the world's barometer was nice, but there was a great emptiness within. No matter how fast I ran, people were always expecting more. No matter how many awards I won, I always wanted more. There was no peace inside, and at times living seemed more like a roller-coaster ride than a rewarding journey. After a year and a half hiatus from running, I decided to make a comeback in 1971. One of my first races back I tied the world record for the indoor mile. It seemed certain that I would make my third Olympic team the next year and possibly even be a favorite to take home the gold medal.

However, in the spring of 1972 I was running 4:10 one week, 3:57 the next, 4:15 the next. In May, I competed in the mile at the Coliseum in Los Angeles, the site where I had set my 1,500-meter world record of 3:33.1 in 1967. Just five years after that feat, in front of a nationally televised audience, I finished dead last, running a 4:19 mile, almost 30 seconds slower than my existing world record in the mile at 3:51.1.

Most who know me say I am a mild-mannered person. But my wife, Anne, found me after the race, outside the stadium, screaming as I beat a tree with my spikes. I was angry, humiliated, empty. I knew I was at the end of my rope, maybe at the end of my running career, and running was my life. I didn't know where to turn.

Shortly after the meet in Los Angeles, Anne and I were playing racquetball with our friends Bernie and Clara Taylor. Afterward we went to the Taylor's for some lemonade. During our visit, I noticed Bernie reading over something on his desk and asked him what it was.

"It's my testimony of coming to know Christ as my personal savior," he said.

Even though Christian friends had faithfully been sharing Christ with me over the years, I didn't quite know what Bernie was talking about. I asked him what he meant, and over the course of the evening, he and his wife shared with Anne and me what it meant to know Jesus Christ as Lord and Savior.

I had been raised in a church and, while growing up, was literally there every time the church doors were open. But I didn't know what it meant to have a personal relationship with a living Savior. That night, it became clear to me what I had been missing in life. It was not about running faster or winning an Olympic medal; those temporal things could never fill the void in me—only Christ could do that. A few weeks later, Anne and I accepted Christ as our personal Lord and Savior. It was the best decision we ever made.

Do you feel empty? Have you ever invited Christ to fill the void?

⚜

Today's reading: Acts 4:12; Romans 3:23

⚜

FREE

Called the "High Priest of the Rebellion" by the British, the Reverend James Caldwell of New Jersey was convinced that God approved of the cause of American independence. Caldwell became a spymaster and was so effective that the British put a price on his head. Caldwell began carrying a brace of pistols, feeling that if he were captured, he would hurt the cause of independence. It was said that no four men alive could take him.

Although Caldwell was a spymaster and an army chaplain, he never missed preaching a sermon. It was said that every Sunday he marched into his church, laid his pistols on either side of the Bible, and delivered his sermons so earnestly that many times he wept. After Caldwell finished his sermon, he would holster his pistols and march back out to his duties in the army.

In 1780, a Tory burned Caldwell's church to the ground and said his only regret was that Caldwell was not set ablaze in his own pulpit. A few months later, the British made an incursion into New Jersey. Caldwell eluded their grasp, but when the British came to his home, they shot his wife to death.

Three weeks after his wife's death, having placed his nine children in the care of a parishioner, Caldwell found himself in the midst of the Battle of Springfield. Seeing a company of American soldiers running low on wadding for their muskets, Caldwell rode to the nearest church. He grabbed stacks of Issac Watts's hymnals and ran back to the American troops, scattering the hymnals among the soldiers.

"Now put Watts into them, boys!" he began yelling.

The American troops began tearing out pages of the hymnals to use as wadding for their muskets. Caldwell's actions helped turn the tide of the battle, and after fierce fighting, the British were driven from Springfield. However, Caldwell would not live to see the end of the Revolution. In November 1781, while helping a friend unload her luggage, Caldwell was shot in the back by a member of the New Jersey militia. Some people contended that the man was bribed by the British to kill Caldwell.[1]

Caldwell's life stands out as an example of Galatians 5:1: "Stand fast therefore in the liberty by which Christ has made us free, and do not be entangled again with a yoke of bondage." Here was a minister who took seriously the idea that Christ had made us free spiritually. Because of that spiritual freedom, we can have political freedom on Earth. Christianity teaches and focuses on an individual's standing before God and how to become free from the bondage of sin and death through Christ. From that understanding of standing before God comes the rights and duties of man: a duty to serve God and develop talents for His glory. Out of the duties and rights comes the desire to create a practical framework by which man can perform those duties and perfect his talents—thus, political freedom.

Caldwell also reminds us that there is a practical application of Christianity to the world around us. Our goal is heaven, but we have responsibilities and duties in this life, at every moment, to be involved in glorifying God in all our actions. We do this best when we are free in Christ.

What does earthly and spiritual freedom mean to you? What affect will your freedom in Christ have on your life today?

❧

Today's reading: Galatians 5:1; Romans 8:1-2

❧

PRESS ON

In his prime, Ron Clarke of Australia was the superman of track. We who were his running peers would often stand back in awe of his tenacity and ability to race night after night. Ron was a long-distance man, running the three-mile, six-mile, and sometimes the marathon. There were times when he would race one night, travel the next day and be competing in another race the next night.

One night he ran a world-class time for the 5,000 meters and the next night dropped down to the mile. Was he exhausted from the run the night before? No, he ran a 4:00.1 mile at a time when 4-minute miles were considered remarkable.

A mark of Ron's incredible strength and talent was his span of races during the summer of 1965. In 16 races, he set 12 world records. In spite of all this, Ron often thought of quitting. Sometimes the pain became extreme. He recounted one race where weariness was beginning to spread through his body:

> My legs became heavier, my chest tighter. Yes, I was getting
> awfully tired, and I had to run with my tiredness . . . the strain
> was telling. The temptation to slow down was almost over-
> whelming. Who wanted a world record anyway? One dreamed,

one planned, one made a schedule, and a record clearly looked possible. But one underestimated the torture.

It would have been very easy for Ron to have slowed or even stepped off the track. So what did he do? "I clenched my fists and flung myself onward." That night Ron broke the world record in the 6-mile run by nearly 30 seconds.

Athletic feats pale in comparison to the apostle Paul's effort to spread the gospel. Yet I have a feeling that he wanted to quit more than once. To be beaten three times with rods, stoned to the point of death once, and shipwrecked makes even the hardest situation, race or workout we face look easy (see 2 Cor. 11:25). Through all Paul's trials, though, never once does he threaten to quit. Instead, he writes to the Philippians, "I press on . . . forgetting those things which are behind and reaching forward to those things which are ahead, I press toward the goal for the prize of the upward call of God in Christ Jesus" (3:12-14). To Timothy he writes, "I have fought the good fight, I have finished the race, I have kept the faith. Finally there is laid up for me a crown of righteousness, which the Lord, the righteous Judge, will give to me on that Day" (4:7-8).

There will be times when we want to quit because life can be hard. However, too many times we quit when success is a moment away. It is said that those who accomplish great things hold on a moment longer when everyone else has let go. When we find ourselves tempted to quit, we need to pray for the strength to continue on. Christ is our hope, and we can do all things through Him who strengthens us.

What is the toughest task, goal or assignment in your life right now? Are you tempted to quit? Or will you press on?

❧

Today's reading: Philippians 3:12; 2 Timothy 4:6-8

❧

I attended the University of Kansas in Lawrence, Kansas (left). While at K.U., I broke the world records in the mile, half-mile, 1,500 meters, and set the American record in the two-mile run. I live in Lawrence, Kansas, to this day.

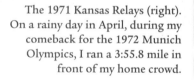

The 1971 Kansas Relays (right). On a rainy day in April, during my comeback for the 1972 Munich Olympics, I ran a 3:55.8 mile in front of my home crowd.

The finish of the 1968 Olympic 1,500 meters. I was the favorite going into the race, but would place second to Kip Keino of Kenya. To this day, having battled a pulled hamstring and mono that summer, and the over 7,000 ft. of altitude in Mexico City, I consider my 3:37 one of my finest efforts ever.

FORGIVENESS

The 1972 Olympics in Munich were supposed to be mine. As a nervous, sick schoolboy in the 1964 summer games, I was eliminated in the 1,500-meter semifinals. In 1968, fighting mononucleosis and the high altitude of Mexico City, I won the silver medal behind Kenya's Kip Keino. Now, in 1972, I was back in peak shape, having run the third fastest mile of all time only a few weeks earlier.

At the start of my 1500-meter prelim, I settled near the back of the pack, knowing that I could easily qualify for the next round. But with 500 meters to go, something went wrong. Another competitor's spike landed on the outside of my right foot, and I stumbled and caught another competitor's elbow in my Adam's apple. When I awoke, I was flat on my back, staring up at the sky. I rose shakily to my feet and staggered down the track, hearing the bell sound, realizing I was 100 meters behind. I finished dead last in my heat, but felt I had been fouled and others told me it was obvious I had been.

A few hours later I sought out my friend Howard Cosell, the famous sportscaster. Howard also happened to be a lawyer, and with a small piece of paper and a pencil, we wrote my protest. It was denied. Coach Timmons obtained footage from a German TV station that supported my claim. Even before the conclusion of the footage, the Olympic officials watching stopped the film and told Timmie there was no conclusive evidence of me being fouled.

Later, an official told me the news that I would not be reinstated. "Mr. Ryun, we are sorry for you, but your protest has been denied and the footage is inconclusive," an official told me. "But you have 1976 to look forward to. Good luck."

It is hard to put in words the anger that I felt at that moment. I wanted to physically beat the Olympic official who denied my protest. But as a new Christian I knew I had to forgive, so I turned and left, knowing deep down inside there would be no more world records, no gold medal.

The setback gnawed at me for years. Some time later, a reporter asked about 1972. I told my story again. But instead of catharsis, the retelling only made me angrier and more bitter. My growth as a new Christian was stunted. I refused to surrender my anger; instead, I clung to it.

One night two years after the event, as I lay awake in bed, I felt the Lord say to me, "Forgive."

I rolled out of bed, got on my knees and said a simple prayer: "Lord, I forgive that Olympic official." The anger and bitterness did not disappear overnight, but it started a continual process of forgiving. I felt like Peter coming to Jesus: "Lord, how many times shall I forgive my brother when he sins against me? Up to seven times?" (Matthew 18:21).

"Seventy times seven," Jesus replied. In no way do I believe Jesus set a number of times that we must forgive; rather, the simple math of that number is so large that it implies continual forgiveness. Four-hundred-ninety is a lot of times to say, "I forgive."

Think of a wrong someone committed against you this week, or in the past, that hit so deep it still hurts. Have you said, "I forgive you"?

❧

Today's reading: Matthew 18:21-22

❧

GRATEFULNESS

Of all people, Christians should be the most grateful. We are the ones who have realized the desperateness of our human condition, who recognize that without Christ, we would be lost. Yet instead of death, we have been offered, and have received, the greatest gift of all, the gift of Jesus Christ. In God's gift we find life everlasting. Are we truly grateful for this gift? We say we are, but is our appreciation exhibited in our daily lives? Does it overflow in a way that people notice? Or do we take it for granted?

When we lack gratefulness, we weaken our character. If we are not thankful for what Christ did for us, we can become introverted, self-serving, unable and unwilling to go beyond ourselves. Ingratitude springs from a selfish spirit in which a person expects to be served, to be the center of attention. A selfish and ungrateful spirit can rob us of the ability to serve others because we consider ourselves above them, or at least we act that way.

Gratefulness in one sense is the realization of where we would be, or what we would be, without Christ. The presence of a grateful attitude should humble us when we see blessings flow toward us. Of course, we should say thanks for the big things we receive that we do not deserve. We should also be grateful for housing, food, clothing—even the morning sunrise and the summer rains. Nothing should be taken for granted. We as Americans have so much that people in other countries only dream of having. To underscore this, each year at Thanksgiving in the Ryun household we sit down and write out a list of items for which we should give thanks. Family, friends, trips, job advancements, blueberry pie, the turkey on the platter—they all make the list. It is a wonderful time of introspection and reflection.

We can thank God for the marvel of eyesight, our taste buds, and fingers that feel what we touch. Consider the miracle of hearing. When I was a young boy, a high fever robbed me of 50 percent of my hearing. The doctors told me the fever's damage would never allow me to gain all my hearing back. Yet several years ago, new hearing aids were developed, and they enabled me to hear things I'd never heard before. One spring day I was able to stand on my porch and listen to the Canada geese fly overhead. It was one of the most beautiful sounds I'd ever heard.

Of course, we all have bad days. When trouble comes along, we struggle with gratefulness. Some days can seem to stretch on in an endless succession of gray tones, with no evidence of joy or hope. During such times, we need to take a moment to deliberately be grateful, even if we don't feel that way.

An old Jewish proverb declares, "If men thanked God for good things, they wouldn't have time to complain about the bad." That is good advice. Gratefulness is a continual thing. It should start with an appreciation for God's gift of Jesus and then flow from there into every aspect of our lives.

Make a list of milestones, gifts, surprises and attributes for which you are grateful. Now add the little things that you take for granted.

Today's reading: 1 Thessalonians 5:16; James 1:17

NECESSARY FAILURE

So often, people fear failure. In our success-driven world, I suppose such trepidation is understandable. But I prefer Herman Melville's approach to failure. "He who has never failed cannot be great," the renowned author once wrote. "Failure is the true test of greatness."[1]

Walt Disney knew failure. He was fired from one of his first jobs and saw ventures end up in bankruptcy before the Disney empire succeeded. Henry Ford also saw bankruptcy before his car-manufacturing business took off.

In 1978, two men were working for a hardware retailer in Los Angeles. When new owners bought the store, they were both fired. The next day a friend suggested they start their own business. Arthur Blank and Bernie Marcus took the advice and started a hardware retail store with high-grade service and a large selection of tools. Today their Home Depot stores are all over America.

Some biblical heroes failed before they succeeded. What would have happened if Simon Peter, after denying Jesus, had never risen from his failure? Let's think about that for a moment. Peter had said he would never desert Christ, but in the course of one night, he denied his Messiah three times. Nonetheless, from that low point of failing Jesus, Peter rose to be the head of the first-century Church. He spread the gospel of Jesus

Christ far and wide, and in the end, when faced with death on a Roman cross, he did not deny Christ, but set an example for us to follow.

We often fail in this life—in relationships, at work, in athletics. We fall short of other's expectations and don't reach our own goals. I cannot recount how many times I have failed in my running, in disappointing those I love, and in serving God. There are decisions I have made that later leave me shaking my head wondering how on Earth I have made it this far in life. How we deal with failure determines whether we go on with Christ or remain stagnate. Are we to wallow in misery or disappointment, or do we learn from failure?

Consider another man's road through life. He failed in business in 1831. He was defeated for the state legislature in 1832. He failed again in business in 1833. He suffered a nervous breakdown in 1836. In 1838, he was defeated in his bid to be a speaker of the state house. He was defeated for Congress three straight times between 1843 and 1855. He was defeated for vice-president in 1856, and lost out one more time for the Senate in 1858. His name was Abraham Lincoln, and he was elected president in 1860.

Jesus Christ calls us to push ahead, to look beyond the failures of this life. We are bound to fail as we pursue great goals. It's human nature. What we must do is conquer the fear of failure, consider it a building process, and look unto Jesus to give us the strength to endure the failure and grow from the lessons we learn through failure.

Think of a failure in your life. What did you learn from it? How can Christ use that disappointment to move you on toward success?

ↄ∫o

Today's reading: Philippians 3:13-15

ↄ∫o

PURE GOLD

Foxe's *Book of Martyrs* records the story of Thomas Hawkes. Hawkes lived in Oxford, England, at a time when Roman Catholicism was the state faith. When Hawkes's first son was born, he refused to have the child baptized into the Roman Catholic Church and would not recant. As a result, Hawkes was tried and found guilty of heresy. A British court condemned him to be burned at the stake.

While Hawkes awaited his death, several friends visited him. These friends, fearing they too would soon suffer Thomas's fate, asked him for some token to show that a man could endure the fire when he stood by his principles without despair. Hawkes promised, "By the help of God, to show them that the most terrible torments could be endured in the glorious cause of Christ and his gospel, the comforts of which were able to lift the believing soul above all the injuries men could inflict."[1]

Hawkes told his friends that when he was being burned, if the pain was bearable, he would raise his hands to heaven before he died. Soon after, the man convicted of heresy was taken to the stake. The kindling was lit, and with a roar, the flames encircled him. Unable to speak, Hawkes stood silent within the flames, his body convulsed in agony. People thought he was dead. Then suddenly, Hawkes lifted his hands above his head and clapped them together three times. Onlookers described it as an act of ecstasy in joy. He soon succumbed to the flames as the crowd stood speechless at his display of courage. His friends walked away, convinced that God could give grace to believers through every trial, even the flames and the stake.[2]

Most likely none of us will ever face the horrors of being burned at the stake, but Thomas Hawkes's story reminds us of God's grace and how He uses trials to refine us. When we face a setback or change, we can ask ourselves, *What is God's purpose in this?* instead of *Why is this happening to me?*

Trials are the furnace that burns away the dross and impurities from our lives. God uses adversity to make us more like Him. Often times, we only see the end results—the beautiful silver necklace or gold ring—but give little thought to the searing fires that brought forth pure metal. Likewise, we laud the great figures of the faith, the apostle Paul, even Martin Luther and John Wesley, without realizing the trials that pushed them closer and closer to Christ. Paul was whipped and imprisoned. Martin Luther nearly lost his life. And John Wesley was beaten by mobs opposed to his teachings.

In the midst of hard times, these great men of faith reacted like Job, who said, "When He has tested me, I shall come forth as gold" (Job 23:10).

Trials either push us away from Christ or draw us to Him. We decide which way to go. I want to be like Paul, Martin Luther and John Wesley, realizing that the trials in this life can be used to deepen my walk with Christ.

How do you react when you face a trial? Does it push you toward Christ or away from Him?

✑

Today's reading: Job 23:10; 2 Corinthians 2:8-10

✑

Salt and Light

Neal Steinhauer was a very fine shot-putter, a literal giant of a man at 6′ 7″ who'd been on several of the national teams with me. After I broke the world record in the mile for the first time, the press hounded me. After hours of interviews, I finally managed to get back to my room and take a shower. A reporter somehow found the phone number for my room and called. Neal was there and calmly picked up the phone. "May I speak with Jim Ryun?" the reporter asked.

"He's in the shower," Neal replied, and hung up.

An hour later, I was of course done showering and was chatting with Neal and a few others when the same reporter called again.

"He's still in the shower," Neal said.

"What? He's still in the shower?" the reporter asked, incredulous.

"He's a very clean boy," Neal replied calmly, then hung up the phone.

Neal was always a humorous man, but most important, he was a Christian. During the spring of 1972, my wife and I and our little daughter moved to Eugene, Oregon, where I could train for the upcoming Olympic trials. Neal was living in Eugene at the time and was leading a Campus Crusade youth group. He invited Anne and me to come to the meetings, which we did, mainly out of curiosity. At the meetings, I would watch Neal teach from the Bible and challenge the young people to live for Christ. I remember having only a faint idea of what Neal was talking about.

I had been raised in the Church of Christ but, due to my negligence and disinterest, had learned very little concerning spiritual matters. As I listened to Neal and the young people talk about Christ with each other, I could see that there was something different about them. They had a peace and contentment that I didn't have, and at that time, it was a peace I desperately wanted.

Several months later, in May 1972, Anne and I both came to Christ. There were many people in our lives who told us about Jesus, but God used Neal to create a curiosity and desire in us that could only be fulfilled by Christ.

Just as Anne and I once did, millions of people recognize emptiness in their lives. Some people attempt to fill it with New Age spiritual experiences, material success or various forms of escapism. Some find temporary peace, but it never lasts. Blaise Pascal once wrote that the vacuum can only be filled by Christ.

In Matthew 5:13, Jesus says, "You are the salt of the earth; but if the salt loses its flavor, how shall it be seasoned?" In verse 14, He states, "You are the light of the world. A city that is set on a hill cannot be hidden." As Christians, we are called to show the way through our words and actions. In my life, Neal was some of that salt and light, and when the time was right and I realized the fruitlessness of my attempts to fill the Christ-void with athletics, his example helped point the way. To this very day, Neal pours his life into others, encouraging, challenging and living a life that has one purpose: to make Christ known.

How are you being salt and light in this world? What are you doing in word and deed to lead others to Christ?

⤝⤞

Today's reading: Matthew 5:13-16; Acts 5:42; 2 Corinthians 2:1-3

⤝⤞

AWAKENINGS

Sometimes Christians forget that Christianity has very practical benefits for this world. We sometimes become lost in what has been termed "platonic Christianity," a focus on heaven without much emphasis on our daily lives. I sometimes joke that if reaching heaven were the only purpose in becoming a Christian, why didn't I get held under water when I was baptized and go straight there? The reason is obvious: Although pilgrims in this life, we are here for a purpose, to glorify God and point others to Him.

When we consider the reformations and revivals of the past, we see an emphasis on practical applications of Christianity. In some ways, reformations and revivals happen when people awaken to the fact that Christianity has very earthly benefits. Consider John Wesley in England during the mid-1700s. Howard Snyder writes:

> When Wesley preached to the Kingswood colliers he was touching those most cruelly victimized by industrialization. . . . Wesley worked tirelessly for their spiritual and material welfare. Among other things, he opened free dispensaries, set up a kind of credit union, and established schools and orphanages. . . . To all these people—the victims of society—Wesley offered the Good News of Jesus Christ. . . . His efforts went beyond welfare to include cre-

ative economic alternatives. . . . He was convinced that "the making an open stand against all the ungodliness and unrighteousness which overspreads our land as a flood, is one of the noblest ways of confessing Christ in the face of His enemies."[1]

During the Great Awakening in America, thousands of people came to Christ and American colonists discovered again the basic truths found in the Bible about inalienable rights and what just and legitimate governments should look like. Some historians say that the Great Awakening gave rise to the generation that made America free.

In the 1830s, the Second Great Awakening swept through America, and again, tens of thousands of people either came to Christ or renewed their faith in Him. Many of these new Christians began to realize that God made all men and women, and that because of that, each one was unique and of inestimable value in His eyes. Out of the Second Great Awakening rose the abolition movement, which forced America to consider the issue of slavery.

We need a reformation today in America. We face issues such as abortion, same-sex marriage and stem cell research. Our culture is at a crossroads.

First, people need to hear the true gospel message found in Romans 3:23: "All have sinned and fallen short of the glory of God" and that "there is no other name [the name of Jesus] under heaven given among men by which we might be saved."

Second, we as Christians need to apply our faith in practical ways to the world around us so that we can show others what it means to "do justly, to love mercy, and to walk humbly with your God" (Micah 6:8). Reformation takes place when Christians apply their faith in their daily lives. When awakening occurs, nations are transformed.

How can you do justice? How can you show mercy in your world?

ℐ

Today's reading: Micah 6:8

ℐ

HERE TODAY

As many Christians know and as was depicted in the recent motion picture *The End of the Spear*, in the 1950s Auca Indians of South America killed Jim Elliot and four other missionaries. Driven by a desire to share Christ with that tribe, those five men were willing to risk and lose everything. Several years before his death, Elliot had written, "He is no fool who gives what he cannot keep to gain what he can never lose."

Those words have since been etched in Christian lore, and thousands of young believers have been inspired to follow in Elliot's footsteps to the mission field. Moreover, we are not fools if each of us, no matter our call or place in life, gives our earthly existence to gain that which is eternal. Let me explain.

I am nearly 60 now, and yet it seems as though just yesterday I was running four-minute miles instead of my present four-minute half miles. At times it seems as though the years pass as days, and before I know it, 10, 15, 20 years have gone by. Indeed, our lives are but a moment in time. As Scripture so clearly and eloquently declares, we are a vapor, like grass, here today and tomorrow thrown into the fires (see Matthew 6:30; 1 Peter 1:23-25).

I have taught my children that we can run fast. We can have successful careers. We can change laws and nations. We can gain everything this world has to offer, but in and of itself, all we accomplish, if done for itself, is meaningless. As the Teacher proclaims in Ecclesiastes, "Vanity of vanities, all is vanity" (1:2). Wisdom, pleasure, wealth, fame, all were vanity to the Teacher because everything the world has to offer is only temporary and can never give lasting meaning. This does not mean we leave behind the day-to-day work and lives we live. It means that we are to do everything right now as unto the Lord, and that we realize it is not for ourselves that we are living, but for Christ.

To use our lives to gain worldly success only would be to squander the greatest resource we have. Adoniram Judson, America's first foreign missionary, wrote to his fiancée, Ann, on New Year's Eve 1810: "A few days and our work will be done. And when it is done, it is done for all eternity. A life once lived is irrevocable. It will remain to be contemplated throughout eternity."[1]

I have made it a goal to live a life worth contemplating throughout eternity, a life lived without regrets, not squandered, but lived for Christ. In all things—work, play, family—Christ must be the aim, living for Him the ultimate goal in all endeavors. I know, I have made this point in several readings, but it is so important that it is worth renewing as our focus each day. Indeed, we are like a vapor, like grass, here today, gone tomorrow. As Jim Elliot wrote, we cannot keep these mortal lives we have been given. Rather we must use them to gain eternal glory.

What work has Christ given to you today? How will you go about that work so that it brings glory to Him?

✍

Today's reading: John 17:16; 1 John 2:15

✍

POWERHOUSE OF PRAYER

In the 1860s, Charles H. Spurgeon built London's Metropolitan Tabernacle into one of the world's largest independent congregations. Almost 6,000 people—including members of Parliament, prime ministers and members of the royal family—would crowd into the Tabernacle to hear the Prince of Preachers. In addition to delivering Sunday sermons, Spurgeon also founded a pastors' college and an orphanage. A prolific author, many of his books went into multiple editions, and 63 volumes of his sermons were published.

Visitors to the Tabernacle often asked Spurgeon what the secret to his success was. In response, he would take them past the massive sanctuary and down into the basement. He would open the door to a prayer room in the basement of the church where people were always kneeling and praying. Then he would look at his visitors and say, "Here is the powerhouse of this church."

Spurgeon himself had the reputation of never praying more than five minutes, but never going five minutes without praying. Spurgeon wrote, "All hell is vanquished when the believer bows his knee in importunate supplication. Beloved brethren, let us pray. We cannot all argue, but we can all pray; we cannot all be leaders, but we can all be pleaders; we cannot all be mighty in rhetoric, but we can all be prevalent in prayer. I would sooner see you eloquent with God than with men. Prayer links us with the Eternal, the Omnipotent, the Infinite, and hence it is our chief resort. . . . Be sure that you are with God, and then you may be sure that God is with you."[1]

Anne and I have prayed together almost every day since we came to know Christ. I recall very clearly a time when we had to pray about our finances. It was roughly the same time when we gave away our last $100 to the church we attended. We literally had $10 in the bank. If we were positive, we could rejoice that we actually still had an account. On the other hand, we could look at our monthly expenses and wonder how on earth we were going to manage.

So we prayed. And we called our spiritual mentors, Clara and Bernie Taylor, and asked them to pray that our needs would be met.

A few days later, our prayers were answered. Post Cereals called and asked me to be a spokesman for a program they were starting in which box tops would be redeemable for playground and sporting equipment. I would begin traveling for them almost immediately. The money I would make from that program would cover all our needs, plus a little extra.

In the bigger picture, our financial needs were hardly earth shattering. But the incident showed me the power of prayer, that as God cares for a sparrow, He also cares for me. It was humbling to get on my knees and say, "Lord, I am yours. You know my needs even before I do." However, praying in this way puts everything in its proper place: God is God, and we are His, who live to do His will. As Spurgeon said, prayer is a powerhouse, but if we're not praying, we'll never know that power.

Is there something you have not asked God about because it would be humbling? Can you ask Him today?

❧

Today's reading: Luke 11:1-4

❧

STRETCHED BY GOD

After living in Eugene, Oregon, for a few months, our family moved to Santa Barbara, California. Being a new believer at the time, more often than not I would drive down to the beach, sit in my car with the windows down and read the Bible. It was on one such morning, sitting in my new Fiat sedan, that a homeless man approached.

"Can you give me money so I can buy some breakfast?" he asked.

Several thoughts flashed through my mind. The first was that I had never seen or smelled a dirtier man. The second was to tell him no. The third was, *How would Christ respond?* I knew better than to give him money, but the man was gaunt with hunger. I knew what I needed to do—drive him to McDonald's and buy him breakfast.

To my surprise, he leapt at the offer, and before I knew it, he was at the passenger-side door. As I reached over to unlock it, I took one last glance at the pristine interior of my car and the clean seats and thought, *Anne hasn't even been in this car yet, and now this dirty bum is going to mess up the seat!*

As I drove to McDonald's, I felt the Lord telling me to share my faith with the man, so I did. It was an awkward, halting presentation of the gospel. People knew I was a changed man since 1972. At times I would mention that I had found Christ and that He had changed my life, but I had not yet shared my faith cold turkey. After buying breakfast for the homeless man, I drove him back to the beach. As he hopped out of the car, I instinctively said, "If you're here tomorrow, let's do this again."

The next morning, he was there and I bought him breakfast and shared my faith with him. The morning after that, he was waiting. Except this time he had several of his homeless friends with him. I couldn't fit them all in the car, so I told them to remain at the beach.

Twenty minutes later I was back with coffee and donuts. Every day for the next several weeks, we repeated the routine. Each morning, the motley crew of homeless men would show up and I would bring coffee and donuts and share my faith. I confess that it stretched me.

Leading a Bible study with homeless men did not come naturally to me. I had grown up as the quiet, partially deaf boy who rarely spoke in public and had found a refuge in running. Now here I was sharing my new-found faith with life's cast-offs.

One day, as suddenly as my new friends appeared, they were gone. I sat for one morning with the coffee and donuts thinking that maybe I had been late. But the next morning no one showed again. I don't know what ever became of those men or if they ever became Christians, but in being faithful to share the gospel, I know I grew in my walk with Christ.

When was the last time God stretched you? How will you respond the next time He asks you to do something that does not come naturally?

❦

Today's reading: Acts 3:11-26; 1 Peter 3:15-16

❦

SPIRITUAL MUSCLES

I sometimes joke that my running career was a success because I had a swim coach who was a former Marine Corps drill sergeant. Coach Timmons was never one to shy away from hard work, and lots of it. His workouts for me, and for my high school teammates, were considered unusual and difficult.

The one that people inevitably ask me about is the 40 x 440-yard workout. "Did you really do that?" some ask skeptically. The answer is yes. To give the workout perspective, imagine running 10 miles on the track, averaging just a shade better than a 4:40 mile pace for the 440s with less than two minutes between each one. We would break the 440s into sets of 10, with a 440 jog in between. Suffice it to say, the workout took hours to complete.

But what people don't realize when they see the number 40 is that Coach Timmons did not have my teammates and me starting at 40 x 440. At the beginning of the cross-country season in the fall, we would begin running 16 x 440, the next week, 20 x 440, the next, 24 x 440, adding four 440s each week until we reached 40. Gradual, incremental stress was added each week, and before I knew it, I was running 40 x 440 yards (which just means 440 yards 40 times), which I could never have done at the beginning of the cross country season. My body had built itself up, and the incremental nature of Coach Timmons's workouts allowed my body to take a great deal of stress, and after a season of so many 440 repeats, I felt I could break the four-minute mile. The next spring, I not only accomplished that feat, but I also found myself on the 1964 Olympic team.

I don't want to give the impression that running 40 x 440 was fun. Running for more than two hours on the same track, in the hot Kansas fall, was not only boring, it hurt, and sometimes I wasn't sure I wanted to keep going. But it made me a better runner. It was like lifting weights—in time, our muscles to respond to the added stress, and we see growth.

I wanted to run a four-minute mile in high school, but I could never have simply walked out of my front door and done that. It took thousands of hours of running—long runs and sprints. It took weight training and stretching.

Sometimes as Christians we attempt to be more like Christ without truly growing spiritual muscles. We race out to do great things for God, but fail to build up our strength. In our walk with Christ, we must take the time to read His Word, pray, and fellowship with others. We must learn to make decisions to live according to His standards of truth and honesty. It's about saying, "Lord, this is for a purpose, and I'm going to keep my eyes on You and respond in a manner that is pleasing to You." When we exercise our faith in this way, we are built up in Christ.

Which spiritual exercise is the toughest for you, reading the Bible or prayer? Can you start out small and deliberately increase the amount you read or time you pray?

⁂

Today's reading: Isaiah 40:29-31

⁂

Sitting in the stands of the L.A. Coliseum after making the 1964 Olympic team as a 17-year-old junior in high school. Going into the Olympic Trials, no one really thought I had a serious chance of making the team. But down the homestretch, I battled from 5th place into the 3rd and final qualifying spot, winning my berth on the Olympic team by a foot.

With my fiancée, Anne, at the 1968 Mexico City Olympics. We recently celebrated 37 wonderful years of marriage.

The moments preceeding the opening heats of the 1972 Olympic 1,500 meters race (above left). After being knocked to the track a few minutes later, I picked myself up and vainly pursued a qualifying spot in the semifinals of the 1,500 meters (above right).

The 1971 Martin Luther King, Jr. Games in Philadelphia (left). I would lose to Marty Liquori (in the Villanova jersey) that day, but run a 3:54 mile. It is still considered one of the greatest races between two American milers.

SUPERMAN

When I was a young boy, I was enthralled with the black-and-white television show *Superman*. Perhaps because I was an awkward, shy boy, I remember wanting to be Superman, to rescue the damsel in distress and save the day.

One day I decided I would be Superman. I went into the kitchen and for some reason decided that I would make a Superman drink that would give me superpowers. With the total belief of a young child, I literally put every liquid substance I could find into the glass, and I added just about every spice I could find in the cupboards. With the naivety of youth, I was convinced this drink would work. I can still remember standing on the back porch with that glass of disgusting substance in my hand. I was not so much concerned with what might happen should I actually drink the substance (like a trip to the hospital to pump my stomach), but as to how I would bank around the trees in the backyard as I was learning to fly. I was also hoping none of the neighbors were watching. If they saw me flying around the backyard, my secret identity would be blown.

Somehow I actually choked down the drink and calmly bent over at the waist, my hands over my head, just like Superman when he was flying. I suppose I was expecting some sort of explosion to come out of my feet that would rocket-launch me into the air, but that never came, and after several minutes, I sheepishly looked around and walked back inside the house, my hopes of being Superman dashed.

The desire to be great, but even more important, to be known and remembered, would grow in me. At one point, while walking across the school yard, I etched my name on a piece of wood and buried it, thinking that perhaps someday, someone would find it and remember Jim Ryun.

It would take many years to discover that no matter how fast I ran, I would never be Superman. At times success was a cruel master, my greatest enemy. There was a period in my career when every time I stepped onto the track, people expected me to set another world record. Sometimes when I won a race but didn't break a record, I was booed. That hurt.

God knows each of us. He knows our strengths and weaknesses, and He loves us. My desire to become Superman, to really be known and remembered, was never truly fulfilled by my running career nor will it be by my political career. It was only fulfilled when I knew that my name was etched, not on some piece of buried wood in a Kansas schoolyard, but in the Book of Life.

We all have an inner desire to be known. As Tommy Walker so beautifully put it in his song "He Knows My Name," we have a maker who knows our every thought and hears us when we call.[1] Indeed, God knows Jim Ryun's name, and that is enough.

In what ways have you sought to be known and recognized? Do you really know that God knows your name?

✍

Today's reading: Psalm 139:13-17; Jeremiah 1:5

✍

HOME RUNS?

In the 1980s, I was a spokesperson for Glaxo Pharmaceuticals. Using as a platform my background as an asthmatic who had not let the symptoms of asthma deter him from succeeding athletically, I traveled around the country, promoting Glaxo's asthma products. As part of the promotion, I signed autographs and had pictures taken with people who stopped by the Glaxo booth.

There was one incident that I will never forget. I was in New York City, taking a lunch break when a Glaxo employee tracked me down. A woman was waiting at the booth. She was excited about getting my autograph and picture. When we got to the booth, sure enough, the woman was patiently waiting.

"Oh, I am so excited!" she said, shaking my hand.

I said it was my pleasure.

"My husband and sons will be so jealous!" she said, as we situated ourselves in front of a display—an oversized picture of me crossing the finish line in the 1972 Olympic trials, of course dressed in running shorts, spikes and a jersey.

"This really is a thrill," she added. "You know, I still remember so clearly all those home runs you used to hit!"

I calmly shook her hand, not entirely sure what to say, and off she went with photograph and autograph in hand. One of the Glaxo employees who had overheard the conversation cracked, "All those home runs, Jim?" We all laughed.

Abraham Lincoln liked to tell the story of an Eastern ruler who once asked his wise men to come up with a saying that would be appropriate for all circumstances. Some time later, the wise men returned. "Do you have a saying that will apply to every circumstance?" the ruler asked. The head wise man nodded: "And this too shall pass."

To this day, I still have no idea who the woman thought I was, but I'm sure when she got home and told her husband she had met the great home-run hitter, Jim Ryun, he had no clue what she was talking about. I still chuckle when I think about that incident, but I think there is a good lesson for all of us in that we should keep a perspective on who we are. In the midst of triumphs or great success, even setbacks and hardships, it's not a bad thing to remind ourselves: And this too shall pass.

I am so grateful for all that I have been given in life and all that I have been able to accomplish with the talents God gave me. But I always want to keep everything in perspective and never think that I am greater than I actually am. Part of keeping a proper perspective on life is to be humble: God gave me the talents I have. They are to be used for His glory, not mine. Part of being humble, I believe, is the ability to not take yourself so seriously and to be able to laugh at yourself.

Think of something embarrassing, humbling or just silly you have done, or that someone has said about you. Are you laughing?

❧

Today's reading: Proverbs 22:4; 1 Peter 5:5

❧

THE FEAR OF GOD

In the 1830s, Elijah Lovejoy began a crusade. An ordained Presbyterian minister, Lovejoy was also a newspaper editor. His editorials for the St. Louis *Observer* constantly addressed the evils of slavery. His stance did not win him many friends in the pro-slavery state of Missouri, but he did acquire many enemies. Lovejoy's printing press was destroyed, he was threatened with physical violence, and in 1836, fearing for his wife and child, he moved across the Mississippi River into Alton, Illinois.

Threats and all, Lovejoy refused to cease his attack on slavery. He changed the name of the paper to the Alton *Observer* and continued writing. Even though he was in the free state of Illinois, his views on slavery were not well received there either. Several more of his presses were destroyed by mobs, and they threatened to tar and feather him. Undeterred, Lovejoy ordered a fourth printing press. However, before the press arrived, the city council of Alton called a meeting to discuss Elijah Lovejoy and his newspaper. After several hours of debate it was decided that Lovejoy had two choices: stop writing his anti-slavery editorials, or leave town.

Lovejoy stood up in that city council meeting and with words similar to those of John Adams he declared, "You speak of compromise. But if by a compromise you mean for me to stop what duty requires of me, I will not do it! The reason is that I fear God more than men! . . . You cannot drive me from Alton, nor can you disgrace me. I, and I alone, can disgrace myself. The deepest disgrace would be at a time like this to deny my Master by forsaking His cause. He died for me, and I would be most unworthy, if I refused, if need be, to die for Him."

I would like to write that the Lovejoy story had a happy ending, but it didn't. Shortly after the city council meeting, as Lovejoy and his friends were trying to defend his new printing press against a large, armed mob, Lovejoy was shot to death. However, historians note that along with the printing of *Uncle Tom's Cabin*, Lovejoy's death was one of the greatest boosts to the abolition movement.

I've thought often about the words "I fear God more than man." I am convinced that whoever we fear the most will dictate how we live our lives. It's not always so easy to decide to fear God. The fear of man—particularly when undergirded by peer pressure—can be a very powerful motivator. There are numerous apples of compromise in life, some leading down easier paths that please men, but not God. Whenever faced with the fear of man, I put it into perspective. Men (and women) can ridicule, humiliate, even kill the body, but they cannot touch the eternal soul. On the other hand, God holds the power of eternity in His hands. He can vanquish both body and soul to the fires of hell. Yes, God is to be feared, but when we fear Him, He responds with love.

Who dictates how you live your life? Who do you fear most, God or man?

Today's reading: Matthew 10:28-31

SEEK FIRST

One of my favorite passages of Scripture is Matthew 6:33: "Seek first the kingdom of God," Jesus commands, "and His righteousness, and all these things [food, drink, clothing] shall be added unto you."

To the young people reading this book, I could not give a better piece of advice. Many youth wonder what to do with their lives, where to go next. When I was 15, I could never have imagined that by the age of 25 I would be a three-time Olympian and multiple world-record holder. People in their teens now certainly have no idea where they will be in 10 years. For that matter, people in their 60s, while having a better idea of what the future might hold, still really do not know the full picture.

Wherever we are, we should seek first the kingdom of God and His righteousness. We should all be able to say, "Lord, I am Yours. All that I have is Yours. Show me Your will and let me seek to be pleasing in Your eyes." Wherever we go in life, we will never regret seeking first the kingdom of God and His righteousness. Scripture clearly promises that God has never left or forsaken His own, and He won't forget each one of us.

We should ask God to give us a vision for our lives. We were each made to glorify Him. We can ask Him how we might use the talents that He has given us to glorify Him. Scripture reads, "Where there is no vision, the people perish" (Proverbs 29:18, *KJV*). In asking God to guide us, we will probably hear back from Him. He might even ask us to do something that we initially think is impossible.

Young people like to take risks. Many of them think nothing of catapulting through the air atop a motor-cross bike or attempting to ride the largest wave in the ocean. Some risk their health with what they eat, their sexual behaviors and their arrogant attitudes. Some risks simply produce a thrill, while others can be downright destructive. We need to know the difference and make wise choices. We also need to know when it is God who is prodding us to take a risk.

Sometimes, Jesus will ask us to get out of the boat and in faith walk to Him, just as He did with Peter. If we hear God calling us to walk to Him but do not leave the boat of our comfort zone, we will miss what God intends for us in that moment. But just as important, if we do not go to Him in faith, we will never achieve all that He has for us.

I am convinced that if we keep our eyes on Jesus, we can, by His grace and strength, walk on water. We can accomplish what we would never have dreamed of doing. However, the kind of faith it takes to walk on water comes only when we seek God first.

Have you asked God to show you His will for your life? What risks is He asking you to take?

⌁

Today's reading: Matthew 6:25-34

⌁

PUSH AND PRESS

There is nothing as wearing or as boring as a solo workout. The workout seems endless. The pain intensifies with each passing mile or repetition. There are times when such a workout is good. It helps build the mental toughness that racing requires. On the other hand, I have always appreciated having a training partner. Working out with another person gives me someone to converse with between sets of intervals and the opportunity to glide behind them as they press the pace.

In my early years of running, I had a blend of both. I would run a solo morning run of five to six miles, and then I would run an afternoon workout with my high school teammates. Often, as my teammates hit the shower, I would run solo workouts where it was just Coach Timmons, the large split clock set beside the track to record my times, and me.

As I matured and my times became faster, I became the world-record holder. My training partners took on new proportions. In preparation for the 1968 Olympics that were to be held at the high altitude of Mexico City, I trained with George Young, Billy Mills and Conrad Nightengale. George was a workhorse, great steeplechaser, four-time Olympian and American record holder. Billy is the only American to ever win the gold medal in the Olympic 10,000 meters. Conrad was one of the finest steeplechasers in the United States. When I ran with them, I was stretched, pulled and extended beyond what I thought I could do. That's the benefit of having quality training partners. They push and press us to better performances.

I went on to capture the silver medal in the 1968 Olympics, running a 3:37 for the 1,500 meters, a time that still stands as one of the best altitude performances by a sea-level runner. For his part, George Young won the bronze medal in the steeplechase. In our respective events, George and I were the first sea-level runners across the line. We had helped each other achieve performances that even one year before would have been impossible.

To me friendships are life's training partners, the push and press of everyday life. Henry Van Dyke once wrote that the mark of a friend is that he makes you wish to be at your best while you are with him. Good friends, like good training partners, pull us forward. They make us better. They stretch us. Good friends challenge us when they see blind spots in our lives. Poor friends have the exact opposite effect—they drag us down. That's why I believe friends are such a critical component to a successful life and are to be chosen wisely. It does matter who we hang out with.

Proverbs 13:20 reads, "He who walks with the wise will be wise. But the companion of fools will be destroyed." Let us be wise people in the company that we keep and the friends that we make.

How has a friend pushed you toward God? How have you pressed a friend further into faith?

∽

Today's reading: Proverbs 13:20; 27:17

∽

STAYING IN THE RACE

One of the most disappointing losses in my career was the 800-meters final of the 1972 Olympic trials. Although I had not run many 800-meter races going into the trials, I was the world-record holder at the half-mile. I knew my main competitors would be Dave Wottle, Ken Swinson and Rick Wolhulter.

My game plan for making the Olympic team was to dominate each round. I figured that if I could get inside my competitors' heads, it might just work to my advantage come the final. I cruised through my first heat, crossing the line in first with a 1:47. In the quarterfinals, I again won my heat with a 1:47. In my semi-final round, I finally faced Dave Wottle. We controlled the race and down the homestretch I eased past him, winning in 1:46.

Going into the final I was confident. I had set a goal for how I wanted the heats to go and they had gone that way. In the final, Dave and I swept past 400 meters in 52.5. I felt good. Probably too good. With 300 meters to go, I made a mistake and kicked early. It was not just an easing into it kind of kick. It was a pedal to the metal, flooring it kind of kick as I whipped past the leaders and roared into the lead. The field instantly strung out behind me as I ran 24 seconds for my third 200. Entering the homestretch, I was still leading. But as the lactic acid set in,

I began to fade. I knew then I'd moved too hard, too soon. The finish line couldn't come soon enough. Dave Wottle ran past me as if I was standing still. Rick Wolhuter slipped past. I saw Ken Swinson working hard on my right. I leaned, but ended up missing the Olympic Team by one-tenth of a second. (Only the top three finishers make the team.)

As I lay recovering on a trainer's table in the infield, half conscious, Dr. Jay Keystone ran over to me.

I did not know I had missed the team yet, so I asked, "Did I make the team?"

"No, Jim. You were fourth," he said.

I don't know why I asked this, but I did. "But did I run a good race?"

"Jim, you ran the best race you could have run."

"Then that's all that matters."

A few days later, I stood at the starting line of the 1,500-meter final. Just like the 800 meters, I had won all my previous rounds. I felt confident, but the failure of the 800 meters was still in the back of my mind. As we circled the track, the laps clicked past—one, two, three. With less than a lap to go, I was waiting patiently just off the shoulders of the leaders. With 300 meters to go, I slowly began to move to the lead. With 200 meters to go, I told myself, "If you go now, you can hold it." And off I went, crossing the finish line in first and making my third Olympic team.

I could have stayed on the table after losing in the 800-meter race, but I didn't. I stayed in the race, and that took courage.

Do you have the courage to stay in life's race?

⌒∽⌒

Today's reading: Galatians 6:8-10; 2 Thessalonians 3:12-14

⌒∽⌒

LEADERSHIP

Some of us are blessed with unique talents. I had the gift to run, and that is something that not everyone is given. I am convinced, however, that all of us can learn skills and qualities in life, and one of those is leadership. The Bible is replete with stories of great leaders, and history tells us of such people as George Washington, Abraham Lincoln and Winston Churchill.

In Exodus, we read of Joshua, the servant and aide of Moses. Here was Joshua, the captain of the armies of Israel and one of the 12 spies sent into the Promised Land. I don't pretend to know exactly what Joshua did in serving Moses, but I'm fascinated by the idea of this obviously strong individual submitting to someone else. Perhaps it began with menial tasks, and as Joshua's responsibilities grew so did Moses' trust. But consider the fact that Joshua served Moses for more than 40 years. When it came time for Joshua to change roles, he was ready to lead the people of Israel into the Promised Land.

In 1 Samuel, we read of David. He was the youngest of seven brothers, and when Samuel came to anoint him, David was in the fields tending the sheep. Being a shepherd and a young boy doesn't seem the ideal place to begin as a leader. But where did David learn how to sling a stone the size of a baseball at 100 miles an hour and hit targets the size of a hair-width? Tending sheep! And when King Saul questioned whether David could defeat Goliath, David responded that he had previously faced fierce opponents.

> Your servant has killed both the lion and the bear; this uncircumcised Philistine will be like one of them because he has defied the armies of the living God (1 Samuel 17:36).

David built up his fighting skills, courage and reliance on God while keeping watch over the sheep. He became a lieutenant of Saul's, one of the most successful war leaders of his day. Later, during the years he was fleeing from Saul, David led a band of men, gaining management skills on a small scale before becoming king over an entire nation.

Also consider Nehemiah, the king's cupbearer who oversaw the construction of Jerusalem's walls. And look at Joseph in his days as a slave and a prisoner before becoming second-in-command over all of Egypt. Joshua, David, Nehemiah and Joseph all began as servants, aides and lieutenants.

One does not become a leader overnight. In many ways, a leader is made stronger by first having served. Becoming a leader is a process of learning to follow instructions, observing the effectiveness or rightness of the direction given, and having one's character molded as difficult decisions are made. Furthermore, role models influence the type of leader a person becomes.

Today we need Christian leaders in all areas of society. Specifically, we need leaders who have a proper perspective on government. They need to be circumspect and well-equipped to engage the world around them.

Who is your Moses—your leader? How have you grown by serving a leader?

⸝

Today's readings: Exodus 33:11; 1 Samuel 16:10-13; 17:34-37

⸝

CLIFF CUSHMAN

Cliff Cushman attended the University of Kansas shortly before I did and in his day he was one of the finest 400 hurdlers in the world. In 1960, he took second in the Olympic Games. For the next four years, Cliff trained to win the gold at Tokyo. But in the 1964 semifinals of the 400-meter hurdles at the U.S. Olympic trials semifinals, he clipped a hurdle and sprawled on the cinders of the backstretch. He didn't advance to the finals.

Afterward, Cliff wrote an open letter to the students at the high school in Grand Forks, North Dakota, where he was a teacher.

> Don't feel sorry for me. . . . In a split second, all the many years of training, pain, sweat, blisters and agony of running were simply and irrevocably wiped out. But I tried! I would much rather fail knowing that I put forth an honest effort than never to have tried at all. . . . Over 15 years ago, I saw a star; first place in the Olympic Games. I literally started running after it. In 1960, I came within three yards of grabbing it (the gold medal); I stumbled, fell, and watched it recede four more years away. Certainly I was very disappointed in falling flat on my face. However, there is nothing I can do about it now but get up, pick the cinders from my wounds and take one more step followed by one more and one more, until the

steps turn into miles, and miles into success. I know I may never make it. The odds are against me, but I have something in my favor—desire and faith. Romans 5:3-5: "We rejoice in our sufferings, knowing that suffering produces endurance, and endurance produces character, and character produces hope, and hope does not disappoint us." At least I am going to try. How about you? . . . I dare you to clean up your language. I dare you to honor your father and mother. I dare you to unselfishly help someone less fortunate than yourself and enjoy the wonderful feeling that goes with it. . . . I dare you to look up at the stars, not down at the mud, and set your sights on one of them that, up to now, you thought was unattainable. . . . You may be surprised at what you can achieve with sincere effort. So get up, pick the cinders out of your wounds and take one more step. I dare you!

Cliff went on to become a captain in the U. S. Air Force and was sent to Vietnam. On September 25, 1966, his F-105 Thunderchief was shot down. He is still listed as M.I.A (missing in action). I sometimes wonder what Cliff might have become and who he would be today. But he was already a great man. Cliff's words, "I have something in my favor—*desire* and *faith*," remind me that the Christian walk is due in many ways to those two character traits.

Are you willing to stand alone, if necessary, and not give in to peer pressure that might lead down the wrong path? (We're all susceptible to peer pressure, no matter how old we are.) God sees you not only for who you are but for what you can become. He loves you so much that He wants you to become all that He intends for you to be.

What is one thing you could work on, in your career or in your walk with Christ, in order to become all that God created you to be?

∽

Today's reading: Romans 5:3-5

∽

MEANINGFUL ENCOURAGEMENT

When I was training in Alamosa, Colorado, for the 1968 Olympics, my physiologist, Jack Daniels, frequently tested me to see what kind of progress I was making in my altitude training. I can still remember doing VO_2 max tests, which were designed to see how much oxygen my body could process. The more red blood cells in my body, the more oxygen I could transfer to my muscles. More oxygen in my muscles meant faster running times.

In Alamosa, Jack was away from his lab and had to improvise how to measure my oxygen level. He would place the VO_2 testing equipment on the hood of a pick-up truck, hook me up to a tube, which would go into my mouth, and block off my nasal passages with a nose clip. When I did VO_2 max testing, I would run to almost complete exhaustion, which was the only way to get an accurate reading.

It was an uncomfortable experience to run alongside a truck at 15 miles an hour, with a tube stuck in my mouth and my nose plugged. But even when I was exhausted, there was no way I was going to stop before the truck did. That tube from my mouth to the truck kept me going. Jack and I still laugh about what might have happened if I had stumbled or passed out. The testing and the discomfort were necessary in my pursuit of excellence as a runner.

In a similar way, it is necessary to have people in our lives, especially spouses, parents, siblings and close friends, who encourage us to keep going in our walk with Christ. A lot of people, when they hear the word "encouragement," think of sports teams and the fans that love to cheer them on. That is one facet of the word "encouragement." Another facet is constructive in nature and can even contain the thought of rebuke. Constructive encouragement is not always a pleasant experience, but it pushes us to do the right thing.

Sometimes meaningful encouragement can take the form of having a blind spot pointed out to us. (I try not to dismiss this kind of constructive "encouragement," even if the attitude of the messenger is less than kind!) What doesn't feel comfortable in the moment can be for our good.

I want to know Christ more and become more like Him. I've learned that part of that process includes people in our lives who will point out our weaknesses and help us move in the right direction. So when someone comes to you with meaningful encouragement for your life, let your first reaction be, "Thank you for pointing that out, I will pray about it," instead of, "You don't know what you're talking about."

Is there someone in your life whose words feel like criticism? If you could identify the kernel of truth in his or her words and interpret them as meaningful encouragement, what would you begin to change today?

✍

Today's reading: Acts 15:30-32; Hebrews 10:24-25

✍

THE ADVENTURE OF LIFE

In May 1996, I carried the Olympic torch through my hometown of Wichita, Kansas. At the ceremony afterward, I was approached by U. S. Congressman Todd Tiahrt and his chief-of-staff, Matt Schlapp. Todd said, "Bob Dole is running for president, and Congressman Sam Brownback is running for his Senate seat. That makes the 2nd Congressional District here in Kansas an open-seat race this fall. Republicans can't afford to lose that seat. Jim, have you ever thought of running for elected office?"

I remember looking at Todd and Matt, thinking, *You've got to be kidding me.* I had vowed years ago to my wife that I would never do two things in life: I would never be a track and field coach and I would never run for elected office.

I politely continued the conversation, thinking that I wouldn't give their idea another thought. But somehow, the idea of running for Congress refused to go away. That night, as Anne and I were driving home to Lawrence, I recounted my conversation with Todd and Matt.

"You told them no, right?" she asked.

"Actually, I didn't. And the idea won't go away. I think it's something we need to pray about."

Anne looked at me in surprise but said, "Okay, let's pray about it."

After much prayer, fasting and consulting with friends, I found myself only weeks later in the state capitol, signing the papers to file my candidacy for the 2nd Congressional District of Kansas. The next five months were a roller-coaster ride of an adventure as my family and I went into full campaign mode. I don't recall the number of meetings I attended or the number of parades or candidate forums, but with the 2nd Congressional District stretching from the Oklahoma border to the Nebraska border, there was quite a bit of travel.

One week before election night, I was down by seven points in the polls. Anne and I had discussed the possibility of losing despite all the hard work, and it looked like a real possibility with only a few days left in the campaign. But I knew, and Anne knew, that we were exactly where God wanted us and, win or lose, we would come away from the experience the better for it.

On election night, we were down early on; but as the night progressed, we closed the gap and then went into the lead. By 10 o'clock that night, I was declared the winner of the 2nd Congressional District and am now in my fifth term in this seat.

Making radical changes has not been my way of living, but I do believe that if God is calling us in a certain direction, then we must be prepared to switch paths even if it seems illogical at the time. God has a plan that many times is well beyond our sight; but He knows the destination.

When you do switch directions, believing that God has called you to do it, commit your whole heart to that path. Life is a wonderful journey, filled with a kaleidoscope of people and experiences that fill our lives and make each experience unique. If we are afraid of the future, afraid of change, then we will miss out on what God has called us to.

Is there a new direction or path that God is impressing on you? What is keeping you from embracing this new adventure?

⌒♫⌒

Today's reading: Proverbs 16:3; 2 Corinthians 5:5-7

⌒♫⌒

In 1996, I started running in a different kind of race. Being a politician is a lot different than being an athlete, but they both take courage. I have come to enjoy campaigning because it is one of the times I get to meet the people I represent.

Former NFL great and Congressman Steve Largent joined me on the campaign trail (above left). After voting for myself in the 1996 congressional election (above right), I knew I would have at least one vote—thankfully a lot of people in the 2nd District voted for me, too, and they have re-elected me as their congressman every two years since.

As a successful athlete, I became quite familiar with media interviews. As a congressman, the reporters still come knocking. At first, there were as many questions about my running career as there were about my politics. Nowadays, I am more often asked about the important issues of the day. Here a local Kansas reporter interviews me in 1997.

We had a great time on the set of Fox and Friends in New York, August 2004. (Back row from left to right is Jim Ryun, Mike Jerrick, Drew Ryun, Ned Ryun. Front row, left to right, is Anne Ryun, Catharine Ryun, Juliet Huddy and Julian Phillips.)

BUBBLES

I loved Bubbles. Small and black, with soft floppy ears, she was the best dog a young boy could have. Every time I came home, there was Bubbles, eager to see me, waiting for a scratch between the ears.

I don't know why I started taking Bubbles on my paper route. Maybe because I saw another paperboy with his small dog tucked in his paper bag; perhaps because I was lonely. My routine became one of walking the two blocks home from my junior high school, grabbing my heavily smudged paper bag, sticking my newspapers in the back pocket of my bag, placing Bubbles in the front of the bag and heading out. My route was about two miles from home, so we'd ride there, I'd lock up my bike and begin tossing papers while Bubbles ran alongside me. I remember my father warning me, "James, I don't want you to take Bubbles with you on your route. She's a small dog and might get hurt while you're out there."

"It'll be fine, Dad," I said, brushing his concerns aside.

Usually when I called, Bubbles was quick to respond. One night, as we crisscrossed the street, Bubbles was a little ways behind me.

"Come on, Bubbles," I called. It was early winter and I was ready to get home.

Behind me, I heard a car coming down the street. It seemed to be moving a bit faster than it should have been. I sensed trouble and suddenly, as the car approached, Bubbles bolted across the street toward me. The driver of the car never saw her. I was devastated, kneeling on the road next to my dying dog. I remember the driver of the car gave me a ride home and on the way there, Bubbles died in my lap.

Believe it or not, for all the success I have had in life, for all the places life has taken me, I still think of Bubbles. I knew my dad did not want me taking my dog along the paper route, but in my youthful willfulness I took her anyway. As I have become older, the story of Bubbles has become for me a lesson in obedience. And as I have grown in my walk with Christ, I realize more and more each day how important obedience is as one of the foundational truths in life. I believe that God does speak to us today. But we should lay all of our requests before Him and then listen for His voice. When we hear His response, we must obey.

The emphasis on obedience is illustrated well in 1 Samuel 15. God, through Samuel, gave Saul clear instructions as to how he was to deal with the Amalekites. Did Saul obey? No! When he encountered the Amalekites, instead of completely destroying his enemies as God had instructed, Saul saved "all that was good," telling Samuel, "the people spared the best . . . to sacrifice to the Lord your God" (15:20).

Then came Samuel's timeless reply, which is as true today as it was when spoken thousands of years ago: "Has the Lord great delight in burnt offerings and sacrifice as in obeying the voice of the Lord? Behold, to obey is better than sacrifice" (15:21).

What is your heavenly Father saying to you today? Are you ready to obey?

❧

Today's reading: 1 Samuel 15:1-35

❧

BEING A FATHER

One of my greatest joys in life is being a father. Although all of my children are grown now and in their 30s, and three are married, it seems as if it was just yesterday that Anne and I had four children who were five and under.

Being with my children as they grew up was a top priority in my life. I would always make breakfast for them in the mornings, and though my skills were limited to eggs and pancakes, we managed. Anne and I also emphasized daily prayer and devotions. Each morning over breakfast, and each night after dinner, we would read the Scriptures together and have a time of prayer. I wanted my children to know how much my walk with Christ meant to me. In addition to our time together in prayer and reading the Bible, I encouraged my children to read a chapter of the Bible every day and have their own time of prayer.

But perhaps some of the best memories I have of my children are from when we traveled together. I was still doing a great deal of speaking and making appearances at road races, and my journeys took me cross country, from Spokane, Washington, to New York City. Because I didn't want the trips to prevent my spending time with the children, Anne and I decided that for most of the trips, I would take one child with me. I have some great memories of those trips. Sometimes it wasn't easy. I remember one trip when I was with my sons and we had a tight connection to make. We were literally on the other side of the airport from where we needed to be, and my sons were only five. So I grabbed a cart, placed them in the seat and I put my old running skills to work, weaving in and out of the foot traffic. I made the plane with just a few minutes to spare.

There are so many wonderful memories of those travel times, and the love I have for my children has grown over the years as I've watched them mature into adults who are walking with Christ. But my love for them pales in comparison to the love Christ has for them. I know it's hard for parents to imagine that anyone could love their children more than they do; but God does. He loves them—in fact, He loves all of us—so much that He sent His only Son to die for us so that we might know eternal life. When I read Isaiah 53:10, and see that it pleased God to bruise Christ and to put Him to grief, for our sakes, I realize that even as a father with my own sons, I can only begin to grasp the beginning of what God has done for us.

I challenge any father reading this to make your children a priority; I've never in my life heard of anyone saying, "I wish I hadn't spent so much time with my children." Often, a parent has deep regrets over the issue of time. So make devotionals and prayer something that you do every day with your children. Never underestimate the value of the 15 to 20 minutes spent every day pointing them to Christ.

What will you do today to make your children a priority and direct their thoughts to the Lord?

Today's reading: Proverbs 3:1-12; 4:1-18

OWNERSHIP

I had almost completed my first year of running, and I was tired. The Kansas winter was in full fury, dumping several feet of snow. Biting wind whipped incessantly through the streets of my hometown of Wichita. Half frozen, I staggered into Coach Timmons's office at the Wichita East Natatorium, the smell of chlorine and the warm, moist air hitting me simultaneously. It was early, well before the start of the school day, but Timmie was already at his desk.

"How are you doing, Jim?" he asked, setting aside his notepad and leaning back in his chair. In the year since I had begun running, he and I had forged a strong relationship. I went from an unknown sophomore to his top runner, both in cross-country and on the track. I was training harder than I had ever imagined I could, all in the pursuit of the four-minute mile.

"Coach," I said, sagging into the chair in his office, "I'm not sure I can do this."

Timmie nodded. "I didn't say it was going to be easy."

"I'm not sure how many more mornings I can get up and run in this weather. It's cold, lonely and dark. The milkman is even telling me it's so cold I could freeze my lungs."

Coach leaned back in his chair, silent for a moment.

"Jim, I can't make you do this," he said. "This is your decision. You have to decide what you want. But I will tell you this. I have never seen a young man with such talent. I think you have the ability to do great things. You've just got to stick in there."

Years later, I would realize that Timmie wanted me to take ownership of the effort. He knew that if I viewed this as Coach wanting me to do it, or if I thought that he was saying *maybe* I could do it, I would view this training as just another thing to do, with no passion involved. During that conversation, I realized that the four-minute mile was something *I* wanted, and I was willing to passionately pursue it, even on cold, lonely mornings.

The next morning, I was out the door, logging a five-mile run through the snowy streets of Wichita. Mile by mile, as I persevered, the training took hold. It wasn't an overnight transformation, but heading into the 1964 track season, I was a new man. Mentally toughened by the hard solo morning runs in the harsh winters of Kansas, I stepped to the starting lines of races with confidence.

We all yearn for spiritual growth, but we want the quick fix; we want it all now. But just as I had to keep training as a young runner, putting one foot in front of the other in that icy weather, we have to discipline ourselves spiritually, putting one foot in front of the other to move toward the upward calling of Christ Jesus. It takes discipline, and it takes time. But it also takes ownership.

If you want to grab hold of Christ and make your walk with Him your own, then start with a daily quiet time to become more spiritually fit, ready for the race of life. When's your next appointment with Him?

❦

Today's reading: 2 Timothy 4:7-8

❦

GREAT MEN

In the United States Capitol, there are statues of some of the great men and women whose lives are an inspiration to us all. The majority of these reside in Statuary Hall, where you will find Lew Wallace, Civil War general and author of *Ben Hur*, William Jennings Bryan, Ethan Allen, and many others. Perhaps the most compelling statue for me is that of Peter Muhlenberg, tucked away near the hallway that leads to the Capitol Rotunda.

Peter was the son of a minister and was ordained as a priest in the Anglican Church in 1772, when he began shepherding the congregation in Woodstock, Virginia. As a pastor, he refused to accept the spiritual-secular dichotomy that existed even in his day, and he became involved in politics. An active member of the Committee of Safety, he was also a member of the Virginia House of Burgesses. On March 23, 1775, he was in attendance for Patrick Henry's "Give Me Liberty or Give Me Death!" speech at St. John's Church in Richmond, Virginia.

On the heels of Henry's speech came a personal request from George Washington that Muhlenberg raise a regiment for the Continental Army. At this crossroads in his life, Muhlenberg faced opposition not only from his father but also from his brother Frederick, who thought a pastor had no business getting involved in political affairs.

Muhlenberg thought otherwise. On Sunday, January 21, 1776, he rose to deliver his sermon, choosing as his text Ecclesiastes 3. When he read verse 8, he said, "There is a time to preach and a time to pray, but there is also a time to fight, and that time has now come." He stripped off his clerical robes and revealed the uniform of a colonel in the Continental Army. After leading his congregation in the hymn "A Mighty Fortress Is Our God," Muhlenberg marched to the back of the church where drummer boys were snapping off a martial beat. It is recorded that 300 men from his church and community formed the nucleus of the 8th Virginia Regiment that day. Muhlenberg rose rapidly from colonel to major general, fighting on the front lines during the battles of Brandywine and Petersburg.

Eventually rewarded with command of Washington's Own, a brigade of crack Continental regulars, Muhlenberg was commander of the American assault on Redoubt 10 at the Battle of Yorktown. When he retired from military service in 1783, he did not feel that he, a military man with blood on his hands, should return to the pulpit. He was elected to the United States House of Representatives four times, joining his brother Frederick, the first Speaker of the U.S. House of Representatives.

I doubt that Muhlenberg woke up one morning and said, "I am going to be a hero." More likely, the small decisions he made every day allowed him to become one of the most celebrated early Americans. None of us can plot the future, saying with utter certainty, "This is where I will be in 10 years." Life just doesn't happen that way. Scripture reads, "A man's steps are directed by the LORD. How then can anyone understand his own way?" (Proverbs 20:24). The key to future success is to let God direct our daily steps and He will guide us to places we never imagined.

What small decisions are you making today that will affect your future in a big way?

❧

Today's reading: Hebrews 11:30-40

❧

A MIGHTY POWER

I love hymns. I grew up in the Church of Christ, where hymns are sung *a capella*. Hymn-singing without accompaniment was part of my first cognitive memories of church, and even though I was 25 years old before I actually accepted Jesus Christ as my Lord and Savior, I believe that all those hymns laid the foundation for my life with Christ.

It's not just the richness of hearing hymns sung or singing them that I love. It is the theology of the Christian faith woven through them. I firmly believe in memorizing Scripture and the Westminster Shorter Catechism, but there's nothing like singing sound theology.

Martin Luther sparked the Reformation with his translation of the Bible into German, and with his hymns. Charles Wesley impacted cultural reformation in England through his 6,000 hymns. It is said of Wesley that while George Whitefield was the orator of the Great Awakening, and Charles's brother John its organizer, Charles was its poet. He and his brother believed that if they could bridge the gap between church and song, they would reach the working masses of England. And they did.

Charles Wesley used the tenets of the Christian faith, sometimes writing as many as three hymns a week, setting the words to tunes of well-known drinking songs of the day. He created songs that the unchurched in England were familiar with and gave them words that taught them about Christ. Wesley described one of the greatest moments of his life as cresting a hill while riding his horse and hearing a young boy singing one of his hymns.

We can learn from Charles Wesley and his brother John. First, they preached Christ at all times. If the pulpits of England were blocked to them, they preached in marketplaces and open fields. They were passionate about their faith. They, like the apostle Peter, were ready in season and out of season to tell others about Christ. Second, they sought ways to bridge the gap, without compromise, between the Christian faith and a dying world through the hymns they wrote. Third, they laid a foundation for future generations through the sound theology of their hymns.

I still remember the times when my children memorized and sang hymns around the dining room table. I chuckle today to hear my young grandsons warble the hymns my daughter and son-in-law are teaching them. There is such richness to hymns like Wesley's "Jesus, Lover of My Soul": *Jesus, lover of my soul, let me to Thy bosom fly, While the nearer waters roll, while the tempest still is high. Hide me, O my Savior, hide, till the storm of life is past; Safe into Thy haven guide; O receive my soul at last.*

And Luther's masterful "A Mighty Fortress Is Our God": *A mighty fortress is our God, a bulwark never failing; Our helper He, amid the flood of mortal ills prevailing: For still our ancient foe doth seek to work us woe; His craft and power are great, and, armed with cruel hate, On earth is not his equal.*

Hymns are so rich with foundational theology that it would be a shame not to internalize their words as part of our walk with Christ. I want to encourage you to sing hymns. If you are a parent, teach hymns to your children and help them ingest rich doctrine in a meaningful way.

What are you singing at your house tonight?

❧

Today's reading: Psalm 98:1-9

❧

A SUCCESSFUL LIFE

In addition to Samuel Rutherford not being a handsome man, he was small and sickly. But for me there has always been something fascinating about Rutherford. Little is known of his childhood. History starts recording his life when he entered Edinburgh College in 1617, at the age of 17. A brilliant student, Rutherford became a member of the Edinburgh College faculty by age 23. However, he resigned in humiliation a few years later due to "fornication with Euphame Hamilton." You could say that he had failed at life

Rutherford's life changed dramatically when he turned to Christ. Like me, Rutherford had been raised in the church but came to Christ years later. He wrote to his friend Robert Stuart, "I suffered my sun to be high in the heaven and near afternoon before ever I [accepted the tender mercies of Christ]."[1] Rutherford, now married to Euphame Hamilton, threw himself into his newfound faith. He sought and received the ministership of a small church outside Edinburgh, and it was said of Rutherford that he was always praying, always preaching, always visiting the sick. Those who knew him best said he would fall asleep speaking of Christ, at times even talking of Him during his sleep.

Rutherford was also a voracious writer—he wrote volumes on theology as well as portions of the Westminster Catechism. But it is his political tome, *Lex Rex*, for which he is best known. And it is because of this book that a price was put on his head by the king of England, Charles II. By proclaiming that God's divine law was king, and the king of England was not law, Rutherford struck at the heart of monarchies, laying the stage for a republican form of democracy.

When he became ill in 1661, Rutherford received word that several of his friends who held to his political views had been executed. He knew that he was going to die, either from his present illness or at the hands of the king's executioner. In the face of that realization, Rutherford told those around his bed, "My blessed Master, He is a Kingly King. And soon I shall shine—I shall see Him as He is—I shall see Him reign, and all His fair company with Him."[2] When the king's messenger came and informed Rutherford that he would be tried and likely executed, Rutherford whispered to the messenger, "Tell them I have summons before a Superior Judge. I behoove to answer my first summons; and ere your day arrive, I will be where few kings and great folk come."[3]

It is the fearlessness of Samuel Rutherford as well as the transformation of his life after accepting the lordship of Christ that inspires me. I believe this fearlessness came from the fact that Rutherford's life focus stayed on Christ. He feared God more than man. Moments before he died, Rutherford turned to his friends gathered in the room and said, "Tell them [fellow pastors] to feed the flock out of love. Tell them to pray for Christ. Preach for Christ. Do all for Christ; beware of man-pleasing."[4] The only point to which the compass of our life must aim is the polestar of Christ.

Is there any area of your life in which you seem to value the opinion of others before you consider first what would please the Lord?

❧

Today's reading: Proverbs 29:25; Acts 4:13-21

❧

A LIFE OF GIVING

In Genesis 15, we read of Abraham's meeting with Melchizedek, the mysterious king of Salem. I am struck by the fact that Abraham gave to Melchizedek a tithe of all he had taken in his recent battle against pagan kings. There was no set amount, no specificity in what was given, just that Abraham "gave him a tithe of all." While we see this same principle a few chapters earlier in the story of Cain and Abel and their offerings to God, it is in the story of Abraham and the king of Salem that I think the principle of tithing is perfected.

Some take the 10 percent guideline from Numbers 18 as a good place for Christians to start when they begin tithing their income to support their local church and its ministries. I think that's a good starting point; but when we adhere to a specific number, we can fall into the trap of saying, "I just gave my 10 percent to God; now I've got 90 percent to do with whatever I want to." The truth is that all that we have is from God. There isn't one thing that does not belong 100 percent to the Lord—our money, our talents, our lives.

The first step toward cultivating a life of giving and tithing begins with this simple prayer: *Lord, all that I have is Yours. Use it and me as You will.* We are to bring the entirety of our lives and lay it on the altar, letting God use us however He chooses. This was a hard lesson for me to learn as a new Christian. It wasn't just about the money, though there was little of that. It was about my life, my running. I thought I had come to where I was in life because *I* had achieved it. Four years after I accepted Christ, I found myself standing in front of the media announcing my retirement from running. "What will you do now, Jim?" a reporter asked.

"I don't know," I said. "But I trust God will guide me. I have given my life to Him."

Giving my life to the Lord is the essence of tithing for me. I am not saying that I'm perfect in this area of my life. We're all human, and we struggle with our humanity every day; but this principle has guided my life for more than 30 years. I believe that with it comes the blessedness of possessing nothing, as A. W. Tozer wrote so beautifully in *The Pursuit of God*. Writing of Abraham's heart transformation after God asked him to sacrifice his son Isaac, and then spared him, Tozer writes:

> He had everything, but possessed nothing. There is the spiritual secret. . . . I think the words *my* and *mine* never again had the same meaning for Abraham. The sense of possession they connote was gone from his heart.[1]

All that we have is God's—our talents, our lives, our families. That mind-set is the secret to being a good steward of the gifts God has given. Part of this stewardship is tithing. He gives gifts to us so that we can use them for His glory.

How do you view your possessions, time, money, abilities, family relationships? In which area do you need the biggest overhaul?

❧

Today's reading: Romans 12:1-2; Ephesians 2:8-9

❧

LIKE A DASH

One of my sons just had his first baby, a little boy he and his wife named Nathaniel Charles, Jr. We call him "Peanut." My son told me about the moment his son came into the world: "All that was visible was Peanut's head. One second his face was still—unanimated—and then he cocked his eyebrow and wrinkled his forehead and took his first breath in this world, let out a cry, and he was so alive."

When I held this beautiful baby boy in my arms, I thought about life and how the passage of time is like grass, here today and gone tomorrow. I once heard a pastor say, "If you go to a graveyard, you see the date of birth and the date of death. Between the dates is a dash. That dash is your life. What are you going to do with it?"

When you look at anyone's tombstone, you can imagine the successes and failures; the lives of children and grandchildren; all the laughter, joy and tears; all the adventures and triumphs compressed into that short dash. At the end of the dash is the date when the person left this world. I think of my grandson's first breath and of the last breaths I've witnessed. Both of my parents passed away, as did my in-laws, and I know that someday I will go the way of all men; it's dust to dust for every man and woman.

Fenélon, the celebrated seventeenth-century French bishop and author, once wrote to a friend struggling with the fear of death:

There is much uncertainty about death, even for the Christian. We are not exactly certain how God is going to judge us, nor can we be absolutely sure about our own characters. But I am not saying this to shake your faith. Instead, I am trying to show you how completely dependent we are on His mercy. . . . But thank God, His mercy is all we need.[1]

Fenélon later wrote, "If we surrender and die to self every day of our lives, there won't be much to do on the last day of our lives. The uncertainties of death will cause no fear when our day comes, if we do not allow these uncertainties to be exaggerated by other worries of self-love."[2]

Thanks be to Jesus Christ, who has conquered death. Anyone who knows Jesus as Lord and Savior can face death with the confidence and assurance that death is just a passage from this life to the next and not the end of existence. Death, as poet John Donne described it, is "one short sleep" and then we shall awaken into eternal life where there will be no more death, no tears or crying, and we shall be forever with the Lord.

We may have no regrets about our lives. Or we may feel a bit panicked when we consider that our time on Earth is like the dash between the beginning and ending dates on a tombstone. But as long as we are still alive, we can choose to live with purpose and make a difference for Christ in the lives of others.

Is there anything you would like to begin changing today?

⌒⌒

Today's reading: 1 Corinthians 15:54-57; Revelation 21:1-4

⌒⌒

FEAR NO MORE

I launched my athletic career not in track but as a baseball player. During my schoolboy days in the 1950s, I was even known to have missed a few days of school due to a "mysterious illness" during the World Series. One of the highlights of my young life was when my father drove me to Curtis Junior High for a baseball outing during my fifth-grade year. It wasn't much—just a small group gathered at the baseball diamond with fielding, pitching and hitting stations set up to test our skills. I was hooked. I practiced as hard as I could for the opportunity to make my church team, and was thrilled when I became the starting third baseman. I had a solid glove and a good arm, but the strength of my game was my batting.

Our first league game, we faced a pitcher that to this day I think was three years older than the rest of us! It seemed like his fast balls were coming over the plate at 100 miles per hour. The bases were loaded my first time at bat, and surprisingly, the second pitch I faced floated over the fence for a grand slam. I don't know who was more surprised—the pitcher or me.

Full of confidence for my second time at bat, I stepped into the batter's box with visions of another home run. I never got to swing at the pitch. Instead, I got drilled in the head and fell to the ground. My head hurt for days afterward, and I began to fear the baseball, not just in the batter's box but in the field as well. I began missing easy grounders and was moved from third base to the outfield and then from the outfield to the bench. That was it for my baseball career. I never played again.

I never really overcame that childhood fear of the baseball, and when I was asked to play on the House Republican baseball team, I had my doubts. This wasn't a slow-pitch softball league. These were members of Congress who suited up in uniforms and played fast-pitch baseball to raise money for charity.

Finally, I agreed to play, but I still remember stepping into the batter's box at my first practice and getting beaned more than 40 years before. But I dug in my cleats and took the first pitch, fighting the urge to step out. I took a few more pitches, and then ripped a single through the gap between the third baseman and the shortstop. It was a small, small victory, but a victory nonetheless.

We all have fears—some big, some insignificantly small. No matter the cause, fear affects the way we approach life. That's why God said, "Fear not, for I am with you. Be not dismayed, for I am your God. I will strengthen you and I will help you, I will uphold you with My righteous right hand" (Isa. 41:10).

We serve a great God, and His strength is sufficient. We can give our fear to God, rely on His strength and go forward with confidence.

Have you ever asked the God of all peace to come into your heart and mind and sweep out a particular fear that has you in its grip?

∽

Today's reading: Isaiah 43:1-5; Luke 12:32

∽

RUNNING CAMPS

On May 18, 1972, my wife, Anne, and I gave our lives to Christ, and we acknowledged a change in priorities. For years, running had been the focus of our lives, the object of my worship. I distinctly remember one of the first Scripture verses that had an impact on us: No greater love has a man than that he lay down his life for his friends (see John 15:13). Anne and I committed to applying this verse to our everyday lives, not just to our own relationship but to our relationships with others as well. The question was, How were we going to do it? I knew that God had given me the talent to run and that my success had created a platform. As much as I could, I wanted to use that platform to share Christ with others.

In 1973, the International Track Association (ITA) was formed. It was a bold enterprise, an attempt to professionalize the sport of track and field, which had been steeped in the amateur code of athletics. Instead of receiving simply a wristwatch for winning a race, now I could walk away with a paycheck. This was important for Anne and me; we had three young children and a fourth on the way.

During the first season of ITA, another organization, called Invest West Sports, was launched with the purpose of hosting various sports camps. As world-record holder in the mile and 1,500 meters, I was asked to work the track and field camps. I agreed, and that first summer of camps was a great success. After several summers of camps, Anne and I realized that while the camps taught the mental and physical aspects, they left out the spiritual component.

So, in the spring of 1976, with only a few dollars in the bank, I launched the Jim Ryun Running Camps. We hosted 30 campers the first summer. It wasn't a great start, but Anne and I loved it and decided to stick with it. The next summer, we had two camps, attracting 40 to 50 campers per camp. By the summer of 1978, we were hosting 4 to 5 camps across the nation. We weren't making any money, and I wondered how we would continue. It was a ministry in the truest sense of the word. Camper's fees covered only the cost and small salaries for the camp staff.

I have great memories from those days. And while we only have one or two camps a year now, they are still going. Some of my former campers are now staffers, and I see a new generation of young runners catching the vision for their purpose in life.

God has given each one of us talents. It may be in athletics. It could be in business. It might even be in writing. We should use the talents and abilities God has given us to bring glory to His name and to point others to Him. There is nothing more fulfilling in this life.

What were you created to do? (Hint: What kind of thing gives you joy in the doing and that blesses others?)

⸉⸉

Today's reading: 1 Corinthians 12:12-31

⸉⸉

The Ryuns meet the president at the Congressional picnic, June 2006. From left to right: Nathaniel Ryun, Catharine Ryun, President Bush, Anne Ryun, Becca Ryun.

Senator Pat Roberts (center) and I chatting with Vice President Dick Cheney aboard his plane after a stop in Kansas.

I never claimed to be a two-sport star, but I do enjoy baseball. Here (insert) I come to the plate during the July 2005 Congressional baseball game. My family (above) joined me on the sidelines.

We had great fun duking it out with House Financial Chairman Mike Oxley at the ESPN Sportszone in Washington, D.C., in July 2002. From Left to right: Ned, Congressman Oxley, Drew and me.

CRISIS OR OPPORTUNITY?

November of my junior year in high school I received an invitation to run at the Cow Palace in San Francisco. The meet directors were putting together a two-mile race for the best high school runners in the nation. Both Coach Timmons and I leapt at the opportunity. Knowing I had never raced on a board track like the one at the Cow Palace, Timmie searched to find one in Kansas. He finally located one at the American Royal Building in Kansas City, which had hosted major events. So very early one Sunday morning, with my parents' approval, a friend drove me to Kansas City where I met Timmie. As we entered the American Royal Building, it was dark and cold; I could see my breath in the dim lighting. To further my dismay, as Timmie and I inspected the track, we noticed that it was not completely bolted together. We spotted two-foot gaps on both the homestretch and backstretch.

I started to protest that it was too cold and too precarious. Timmie (who was almost a foot shorter than me) looked up and said, "Jim, that track in San Francisco is a board track. You need some experience on one—it's not like running on a cinder track. This is a great opportunity to get a feel for one. Get warmed up and let's go."

After a good warm up, I stripped down to my shorts and tank top, laced my spikes up and trotted to the starting line. Timmie played the role of starter, and off I went for 24 laps. I can't remember the time of that solo run, but it gave me valuable experience for the race at the Cow Palace, where I placed second.

In life, we are often faced with situations where the circumstances are hardly ideal. I realize running a solo time trial in a cold building on an incomplete board track is a very minor predicament in the big scheme of things, but I still remember Timmie's words: "This is a great opportunity." This reminds me of Joshua and Caleb when they returned with the other ten from spying on the Promised Land. The ten said to Moses and the people, "There are giants in the land, we can't do this." Joshua and Caleb said, "This is an opportunity for God to show Himself strong on our behalf" (see Numbers 13—14).

It also reminds me of David and Goliath. King Saul and the army of Israel saw Goliath as a major crisis. David saw fighting him as an opportunity for God to win a great victory, so he declared to Goliath, "The battle is the Lord's, and He will give you into our hands." In Acts 27, the apostle Paul, bound in chains and on a ship battered by the seas, saw his circumstances not as a crisis, but as an opportunity to declare the sovereignty of God. Even after the ship was crushed on the shores of Malta, Paul still saw his circumstances as an opportunity to further the gospel. Bitten by a viper while gathering firewood, Paul shook the snake off and then went on to hold a prayer and healing service.

What crises have you faced this week? Are they actually opportunities?

⨎

Today's reading: Numbers 13:21-33; 1 Samuel 17:19-51

Acts 27:13—28:10

⨎

GODLY GENERATIONS

Anne and I have always prayed for our children. We came to Christ a year after our first daughter was born. But since then, we have literally prayed for our children from the time they were still in the womb. Our prayers were that they would come to know Christ. We also prayed for their future spouses (three are married now, and we're praying for the fourth spouse to come). And we prayed that they would be used to glorify God.

We challenged our children to have a vision for their lives—the most important vision being that they would glorify God in everything they do, in whatever direction He would lead them. We challenged them to think beyond the present and to consider more and greater things than simply what lay before them day by day.

Today my youngest daughter, Catharine, works at the White House in the Faith Based and Community Initiatives Office. My son Ned worked there as well, as a presidential writer, and he's now the head of a national organization called Generation Joshua, whose mission is to encourage Christian youth to become involved in the civic and political arenas. Passing along a vision to young people so that they can impact the world for Christ is an exciting mission to me.

My other son, Drew, worked as the national director for social conservatives at the Republican National Committee and now directs government affairs for the American Center for Law and Justice.

I now have four grandchildren: Justus, Walker, Mercedes and Nathaniel Charles, Jr. (Grandchildren five and six are on the way!) Anne and I pray for our grandchildren as well, and I can't help but smile when I hear a young voice on the other end of the phone line telling me what he's learned that day.

Sometimes I'll ask, "Who made you?"

"God."

"What else did He make?"

"Everything."

My hope has always been that my children, my grandchildren and those who come later will come to Christ, love God for all their days and seek to serve Him, and that they will impact the world for Christ. That's why we are here: to glorify God and to point others to Him through Christ so that the whole earth might be filled with His glory.

Have you experienced what it means to glorify God by "enjoying" Him (finding your greatest satisfaction in who He is and the fact that He is your God and Redeemer)? What could you do to cultivate this understanding in a deeper way, not only in your heart but also in the hearts of your children so that they will do the same for their children and pass on God's renown? What is just one way you could begin to invest in the next generation so that they will desire to glorify God through their lives?

❧

Today's reading: Psalms 22:30-31; 100:1-5

❧

THE MARATHON LIFE

Life with Christ is not a 100-meter sprint. It is a marathon, with hurdles, hills and valleys along the way, each challenge uniquely situated to help us grow in our walk with Christ.

I trained hard to become the best miler in the world. Even though my rise from a gawky 15-year-old to a world-record holder was meteoric by most standards, it did not happen overnight. I didn't just roll out of bed one morning and say, "I'm lacing up my shoes, stepping out the door and running a sub-4-minute mile." My rise began first with a goal. Then came a plan, step by step how I was going to achieve my goal. It took a focus previously unknown to me. But the road to success was not without bumps. There were injuries, delays and incredible physical and mental exhaustion.

Here is a brief recap of what a year of training looked like. During the fall months, I focused on base mileage, developing the ability to handle greater workloads than ever before. Sometimes that meant logging 120 miles of running a week.

Near the end of the fall season, I'd begin hardening my system for races through added emphasis on interval training, a lot of which was 400-meter repeats run at a 60-second pace with 60 seconds rest. Those were tough workouts, especially as they always followed a 5- to 6-mile run in the morning.

As I began to prepare for the actual racing season, I worked in more speed work, blasting through sub-50-second 400-meter repeats or rattling off 200s in 23 seconds. In short, I just didn't show up at the starting line of a major competition, nor did I casually run a few miles every day or simply think about how fast I wanted to run and hope for the best. There was a step-by-step plan and a dedication to complete it.

While I am not saying that the walk with Christ and running are identical in their applications, I am suggesting that running provides lessons for our lives with Christ. Just as I trained my physical body to be the best, I also see that we as Christians need to train our spiritual man.

I like to think of daily reading of God's Word as the base training of our spiritual lives. Reading a few verses here and there will not do it. We need mass absorption of God's Word—reading chapter after chapter each morning.

Our interval training is Scripture memorization. Just as interval training was always the toughest component of my physical training, Scripture memorization can be the toughest component of spiritual fitness. I am amazed every year at my running camp when one of our counselors, Marc Dick, quotes chapters of the Bible during his morning devotionals. How does Marc do it? "I've got a plan," he explains, "and I stick to it."

We must not stop at reading and memorizing God's Word. If we do not cross this bridge from reading and memorization to actually meditating on what we read and thinking about how it applies to our lives, we can never reach the deepest and greatest life Christ has for each of us.

Do you have a Bible-reading plan? How often do you cross the bridge from reading and memorization to meditate on God's Word?

⚏

Today's reading: Psalm 119:11; 2 Peter 1:6

⚏

GOOD INVESTMENTS

In the parable of the talents in Matthew 25, the master goes away, leaving three servants with varying amounts of money (talents). Scripture does not indicate what the master wanted done with his money; he simply gives according to each servant's own ability. The first servant doubles his five talents to ten; the second doubles his to four. The final servant, however, buries his one talent in the ground. When the master returns, he rewards the first two servants, but the final servant is derided as wicked and lazy and cast into outer darkness. I am struck by the concept of stewardship, and how the master responded to how each servant handled his responsibility. Such reflection stirs me to ask myself, *How can I be a good steward?*

Too often in America we take for granted our freedom and prosperity. At the risk of sounding jingoistic, we have the greatest constitutional republic the world has ever known. Many other stable nations have gone through dozens of constitutions over the last 200 years—America has remained under the same constitution since the 1780s. We have freedoms only dreamed of in many countries: freedom of religion, freedom of speech, freedom of the press, freedom of assembly, and freedom of petition. We have the right to elect our own leaders. In an age of monarchy when the Founders wrote those rights into out Constitution, they were radical freedoms. Where did our founders find the inspiration for such a form of government that guaranteed such freedoms for its citizens?

A study conducted in the late 1970s researched more than 15,000 documents of the founders to determine what inspired them. The most frequently cited source by our founders was the Bible, followed by Montesquieu, Blackstone and Locke—men who moved within a Judeo-Christian worldview.

There are many benefits to our government. One I like to consider is the Mayflower Institute's estimate that America, over the past 200 years, has provided 80 to 85 percent of the gospel message and resources to the world, and we only represent roughly 5 percent of the world's population. The freedoms given to us have provided a fertile ground for the spreading of the gospel.

America has been a city on a hill, but recent culture struggles have attacked the foundation of our nation. How long can a nation survive that has abortion as the law of the land and questions the definition of marriage? We have prospered as a nation, but if our worldview continues to turn for the worse, how long will we continue to be good stewards and leaders in sharing the gospel?

We must have a culture of life, and one where marriage is protected—otherwise our position as a city set on a hill will be in jeopardy. We will risk burying rather than investing the talents God has given us, as a nation and as individuals. Someday our Ruler will return and ask what we have done with our talents. We will be called to account for how we have handled our wealth, our influence and our time—our lives. The question will be, What kind of stewards have we been?

What talents has God given you? How will you invest them today?

❦

Today's reading: Matthew 25:14-30

❦

WORLDVIEW WAR

We live in a culture of competing worldviews. By worldview, I mean a foundational set of suppositions, values and biases by which each individual views the world about him or her and by which he or she makes decisions. It is the set of glasses through which each individual sees the world.

For those of us who call ourselves Christians, we believe in one, tri-une God who created heaven and Earth. We believe that He sent His Son, Jesus, to die for our sins and it is only when we accept Christ's work on the cross that we are justified. We believe that God's Word, the Bible, is divinely inspired and is the foundation for the decisions that we make in our everyday lives. Because of this, we believe in absolute truth.

Within the public arena, we face an opposing worldview. It is a post-modern, relativistic, humanistic worldview where man is the measure of all things. When we take a look around, this worldview stares right back at us. Humanism is diametrically opposed to all that we as followers of Christ believe in. And as such, it aggressively seeks to win the war of ideas in the arena. Culture, society and politics do not exist in a static vacuum. There is constant struggle between the two worldviews. One side wins, one side loses and ideas have consequences.

There are some in the Christian community who say, "We've no business being involved in culture and politics." They have a right to their opinion, but I believe while we are not supposed to be of this world, we are called to live in it. I believe that when Jesus said to go out into all of the world, He did not mean *just* the geographic world. He meant the worlds of education, the arts, science, politics and business. In Luke 19:13, Jesus gives us a direct command, "Occupy until I return." It is an individual command to each one of us. I like to think of it in this way: "You occupy in the place I have called you until I return."

God has given each one of us unique talents. We are called to use them in the place where Christ leads us. To simply avoid the obvious and ignore the world around us is to vacate our rightful place in the arena. Christ has called me into politics. He has called others into education, to be the best teachers they can be. And some He has called into business, to be the best businessmen they can be. We have an obligation to pursue excellence because it is a witness for Christ.

Our worldview dictates the decisions we make. If we believe God created us, then we believe we have inherent worth. If we believe random selection somehow plopped us down on this Earth, our view dictates the conclusions we come to when faced with decisions in life. As one of my peers in Congress says, it is a sense of situational awareness. We need to know our worldview, and then enter into the arena.

What is your basic worldview? Have you entered the arena?

⚬✌🏻⚬

Today's reading: Proverbs 4:5-7; Ephesians 5:15-16; James 1:5

⚬✌🏻⚬

No One Sees

I have always loved golf. I remember the days when my young friends and I would take old, hand-me-down clubs and play on the municipal course in Wichita, Kansas. We were truly horrible and had no clue about the rules of the game. I still remember how we'd tee the ball up in the fairway for our second shots. We figured if you could tee it up on the tee box, you could tee it up on the fairway as well.

During my running career, I golfed periodically, but played more and more as I began dating Anne—her dad and brothers were dedicated golfers. Some of my fondest memories with my father-in-law, Moose Snider, are those spent on the golf course. My career opened doors to play on some wonderful courses, such as Pebble Beach, where Moose, Ned, Drew and I played one of our last rounds together. I think that's one of the reasons I love golf so much—it is both a competitive and a social sport.

As the years have progressed, I still golf. In recent history, I shocked my House golfing peers as I halved my match in the annual Democrat versus Republican Cup match. But I am nowhere near as good as I would like to be. The fine motor skills of golf that only come by continual practice are beyond me. When I break 40 for 9 holes, a small celebration takes place.

I think what I love most about golf is the life lessons it teaches. When I break golf and running into separate categories, I think of running as a discipline that teaches perseverance, dedication, physical training and mental toughness. It's at the mental level that running and golf intersect. Golf is a game that stresses mental toughness. It is wearing to hit a beautiful drive, then shank an approach shot out of bounds or into a sand trap. It is discouraging to hit a green in regulation, then three-putt a par away (just bear with me if you are not a golfer, this makes sense to anyone who plays!). Like running, golf gives you the ability not only to beat other competitors, but also to win the battle between the ears. Golf teaches integrity and an adherence to rules even when no one else is watching.

Trust me. It is easy to adjust the ball to a better lie when no one is watching, or drop another ball and take a mulligan or take a putt even though it's still five feet from the hole and justify it with, *Yeah, I can hit that putt.*

It's not too far a stretch to apply golf lessons to life. It's much easier to think, *I don't have to do this excellently because I'll get a mulligan.* In life, there are few mulligans and when we do get them, they are a gift from God. There are a lot of times when we think no one is watching and we "adjust" our lie in life, tweaking the facts, thinking we will *get away with it.* But that is not living a life of integrity.

What we do when no one else is watching defines who we really are. When we do the small things excellently, with integrity, we can then watch how far we will go in life.

When was the last time you "cheated" when no one was looking? How will you respond when tempted again?

Today's reading: 1 Samuel 16:1-7; 1 Peter 2:11-12

A SOVEREIGN GOD

Some people call the founding fathers of the United States of America nothing more than atheists, deists, agnostics and opportunists. A brief look at history paints a different picture.

The Reverend Dr. John Witherspoon, president of the College of New Jersey, was an ordained minister who signed the Declaration of Independence. Having 20 volumes of his sermons printed and published throughout the colonies, Witherspoon was one of the most popular ministers in early America. Samuel Adams also signed the Declaration of Independence. Moments later he said, "We have this day restored the Sovereign to Whom all men ought to be obedient. From the rising to the setting of the sun, let His kingdom come."[1] Roger Sherman, who began life as a humble cobbler and rose to be a U.S. Senator, was one of the five men who actually helped draft the Declaration. Sherman also wrote his church's creed:

> I believe that there is one only living and true God, existing in three persons, the Father, the Son, and the Holy Ghost . . . that God did send His own Son to become man, die in the room and stead of sinners, and thus to lay the foundation for the offer of pardon and salvation to all mankind so as all may be saved who are willing to accept the Gospel offer [and] that at the end of this world there will

be a resurrection of the dead and a final judgment of all mankind when the righteous shall be publicly acquitted by Christ the Judge and admitted to everlasting life and glory, and the wicked be sentenced to everlasting punishment.[2]

Witherspoon, Adams and Sherman are only a few examples of the hundreds of men who are considered founders of this great nation. Although it would be disingenuous to call all of our founders Christians, it can be said with a certain degree of certainty that most moved within a Judeo-Christian worldview. In fact, despite what some revisionists purport today, Americans in the founding era expected, almost demanded, that their leaders adhere to a Christian perspective while in the public arena, even if some privately did not believe in God.

It concerns me that we are losing the knowledge of this rich heritage and changing the facts of the past. If we do not know where we have come from as a nation, we cannot know where we are going. The knowledge of what has made us a great nation will help guide us into the future. On the other hand, if we allow secular humanists to rewrite history, we become unstable and susceptible to propaganda, lies and whatever feels good at the moment.

Think for a moment about how this impacts our lives each day. A belief in one sovereign God shapes our values, morals, business decisions, educational priorities and laws of the land. Just one example for today: With a sovereign God, we know that all men and women are equal in His eyes, therefore we will make decisions, set priorities and establish laws that value the individual. Without a sovereign God, a survival of the fittest, smartest or wittiest could prevail.

How will the existence of a sovereign God affect the decisions you make today?

⌘

Today's reading: Deuteronomy 6:4-9; Mark 12:28-34; 1 Corinthians 8:4-6

⌘

A STAND

There is power in the ability to formulate an idea and take a stand. People who can do this—independent thinkers—sometimes must stand up to "group think." Group think happens in classrooms, businesses and churches. I frequently see it in Washington, D.C. By nature, humans choose the path of least resistance, and it is far easier to go along to get along than it is to stand alone against the way many people think that something should be done.

Standing alone is not popular, nor is it easy. For me, a little-known prophet from the Old Testament named Micaiah is a model of how to stand up to group think. We read about him in 1 Kings 22. Let's set the scene: Ahab, king of Israel, and Jehoshaphat, king of Judah, are discussing whether they should go to war against the Syrians. Jehoshaphat asks, "Please inquire for the word of the Lord today." I envision Ahab clapping his hands and, on cue, 400 court prophets trot out. Ahab asks the prophets, "Shall I go fight?" In unison, they answer, "Go, the Lord will give you the victory."

Next comes the classic line from Jehoshaphat: "Is there not still a prophet of the Lord here that we may inquire of him?" Into this scene of prophetic group think strides Micaiah, a man despised by Ahab. "Shall we go to battle?" the king asks. I can almost see Micaiah look at the crowd of court prophets before him, knowing what they've said and then turn to Ahab, "Go, the Lord will give you the victory." To which Ahab replies, "How many times shall I make you swear that you tell me nothing but the truth in the name of the Lord?" Then Micaiah says, "I saw all of Israel scattered on the mountains, as sheep that have no shepherd." He then turns and rebukes the 400 court prophets, saying a lying spirit speaks through them.

For his pains, Micaiah was thrown into prison by Ahab. I love this story because it speaks to our humanity. Note Micaiah's first answer that leads us to think that he intended to just go along to get along. All of us will, at some point in our life, face the same crossroad. Believe me, I have been in meetings when I was tempted to say yes when I really disagreed.

As for Micaiah, in the end he stands and speaks what God has told him. It is straight to the point: Ahab, if you go to battle, you will die and Israel will be scattered. As one who is in leadership, I value those who approach problems from different angles than I do and are unafraid to speak their minds.

A good disagreement helps formulate great ideas and leaves good ones by the wayside. Scripture tells us, "In the multitude of counselors there is safety" (Proverbs 11:14) and "by wise counsel you will wage your own war" (Proverbs 24:6). The writers of the proverbs are not referring to the comfort of group think or of leaders who surround themselves with yes people. They are referring to the arena of ideas, the different angles of thought that wise people bring to the table.

Think of a time when you went along with the group and succumbed to group think. What can you do differently next time to take a stand?

☙

Today's reading: 1 Kings 22:1-28; Philippians 3:17-21

☙

A SIMPLE ACT

Abraham Kuyper, the Christian prime minister of the Netherlands in the early twentieth century, once spoke on what he viewed as the three stages of the Christian life. To Kuyper, the first stage begins with the conversion to Christ, with the new Christian sometimes still entangled in worldliness. The second stage is one in which the new Christian turns away from worldly cares to meditate on Christ. Kuyper warned, however, that in the second stage, many Christians fall into a false mysticism. The third stage is one of greater maturity and balance in which the believer realizes that everything is from the Lord, and thus in everything His name must be glorified.

In his speech, Kuyper pointed out that the evangelical Christian remaining in the second stage feels that politics are to be avoided as corrupting and ungodly. To Kuyper, however, those Christians give over their legitimate responsibilities in the civic and political arena to the control of secular humanists.

I sense that some Christians still get trapped into a mind-set that unless we are doing something overtly spiritual, we are somehow spiritually immature. I've even heard Christians say, "Christians don't belong in politics" or "The words 'godly' and 'politician' don't belong in the same sentence; politics is a moral cesspool." My initial response is,

"Where there is no salt and light, there will be decay." My thought also is that Christ has called me personally to the political arena, and for now, this is where I am supposed to be. Within that understanding, I can make my career in politics an act of worship by being a man of integrity, honesty, justice and mercy while walking humbly with Him.

Christ has called us to go into the entire world—not just our fellowship group. The whole world can mean the mission field or seminary. It can mean law, business, medicine, media, the fine arts, sports—even politics. Lord Ashley Cooper, 7th Earl of Shaftsbury and a member of Parliament in the mid-1800s, once told a friend, "I think a man's religion, if it is worth anything, should enter into every sphere of life, and rule his conduct in every relation. I have always been, and please God, always shall be, an Evangelical."

Some people are called to be missionaries in Cambodia, Romania or Paraguay. Some are called to be salt and light at the grocery store, school or recreation department just down the street. We can love and serve Christ by feeding children in Africa or by painting the widow's house next door. Both are equally important, as long as that is what God has called us to do. We can, in our daily lives, make even the driving of a taxi, the running a race, or the cleaning of a bathroom a simple act of worship to Him who created us. I can do that by actually worshiping as I drive my car, run to stay in shape, clean my house, vote in Congress, and meet with my staff. We can all make our lives ones of devotion and worship by living lives that are pleasing to Christ and glorifying to Him.

What's on your to-do list today? How can you make each item an act of worship?

❧

Today's reading: 1 Corinthians 10:31

❧

CHARACTER AND DESTINY

In Genesis, we read of Joseph. I'm sure most are familiar with the story, but here was a young man who dreamed of greatness, that someday his brothers, even his father, would bow before him. Joseph was convinced of his future success, and in his immaturity, informed his brothers of that fact.

Call it sibling rivalry if you want (something my sons, who helped me write this book, *never* have—ha!). Joseph's brothers sold him into slavery, and Joseph found himself not on the road to greatness, but as a slave in the house of Potiphar. How did Joseph respond? He remained faithful to God. When approached by Potiphar's wife, Joseph rejected temptation, and for his troubles was thrown into prison. So he went from being the heir of an important man to being a slave and then a prisoner. Sounds to me like Joseph was going the wrong way.

I sometimes wonder if in the back of Joseph's mind, doubts began to creep in. Perhaps he even wondered if the dream was from God. Yet he did not shirk or shrink away from the difficult times. Instead, he embraced the challenge.

The forging of Joseph's character reminds me of the story of how samurai swords are made. The sword maker sometimes spends months creating one sword, beating almost 33,000 thin pieces of metal into one sword, plunging the sword into the fires, beating the metal, plunging it into water, then into the fires again. Sometimes the sword maker repeats the process of beating and plunging the sword into the fires 30 times. In the end, the sword is a masterpiece, not only beautiful to behold, but effective in a fight—with willow-like flexibility and a razor's edge. However, the sword would not be of such high quality without the fires and without the hammer. So it is with our character: Without challenge, our character will never grow and we will never become all that we should be.

When Joseph is finally remembered and brought before Pharaoh to interpret Pharaoh's dreams, Joseph is suddenly lifted, in almost a moment, from being a prisoner to being the second-in-command of all of Egypt, one of the world's superpowers at the time. Joseph immediately enacts a plan to avert disaster from the impending famine, and ultimately achieves the greatness he'd dreamed of so long before.

I am convinced that when character and destiny meet, greatness results. I believe that in many ways destiny is a choice, but sometimes, as with Joseph, it comes upon us suddenly. What if Joseph had shrunk back from the trials in his life? And not just from being a slave, but also from going even a step lower to being a prisoner? He would not have been ready for the destiny God had for him.

I believe that God places challenges in our lives to make us more like Him and to develop character. We must not try to avoid the hard times. To shrink back from them is to not allow ourselves to grow. God has placed them in our path for a reason. When we embrace adversity, our character rises to the level necessary to meet our destiny.

When you face adversity, do you recoil or embrace the hard times? How might God be using a challenge in your life right now to shape character in your life and to enable you to reach your destiny?

❦

Today's reading: Genesis 37:1-36; 39:1-23; 40:1—41:57

❦

Anne and I leaving for our honey-moon on our wedding day (above), January 25, 1969. The picture was taken in front of my in-laws' home in Bay Village, Ohio.

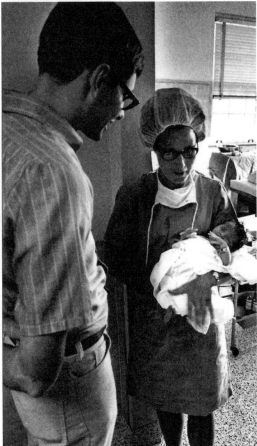

Amazing! This was the day my daughter Heather was born, June 21, 1970, in Topeka, Kansas (right).

Through the years, I have enjoyed passing on to others what has been given to me. One way I do this is through my Jim Ryun Running Camp. My camp is unique in that the instruction is geared toward developing the total runner: physically, mentally and spiritually. Here is the 2004 staff, from left to right: Coach Bill Lundberg, Ryan Hall, Catharine Ryun, Ned Ryun, Anne Ryun, Simon Maher, Jim Ryun, Marc Dick, Walker Tiffany, Justus Tiffany, Heather Tiffany, Dr. Jack Daniels, Heidi Fuhrman, Daymen Tiffany, Mercedes Tiffany and Scott Keenan.

Most of our clan back in Lawrence, Kansas, June 2006. From left to right: Justus Tiffany, Daymen Tiffany, Anne Ryun, Mercedes Tiffany, Heather Tiffany, Jim Ryun, Nathaniel Ryun, Ned Ryun, Becca Ryun, Walker Tiffany.

REFLECTIONS ON COURAGE

OVERCOMING FEAR

STANDING FIRM

MAKING THE SACRIFICE

OVERCOMING FEAR

NED RYUN

Mark Twain once wrote, "Courage is the resistance to fear, mastery of fear—not the absence of fear." For without fear, there could be no courage: Courage is the decision to stand fast in the face of fear. It is the decision to rise to the challenge of fear and not to retreat that makes heroes.

Every day we face fear: fear of failure, fear of rejection, ridicule, perhaps even physical pain or death. Yet where do we find the strength and the will to face those fears? What is it that drives us to move forward and confront those fears instead of fleeing from them? How have men and women throughout history faced the flames and the stake, the firing squad, beheadings, and being tortured to death? How did the Christian stand in the sandy Coliseum, alone in the arena before the screaming, pulsating mobs as the lions moved closer, knowing that to recant was to live? And yet there was no recantation, only a horrible death at the teeth of the beasts because the Christian knew that there was something more, that there was something better, and that the pain of the moment was nothing in the light of eternity.

Courage for the Christian is in many ways related to the fact that God is; for out of the Eternal spring Goodness, Rightness, Justice and Love, and if God exists, then those ideals must. It is this belief that gives us the ability to hope, which gives us the courage to face our fears because we know that even in the face of suffering, fear and death we can rest in peace. Even though we might walk through the valley of the shadow of death, we can know that it is only the shadows we face, and that eternal death cannot touch us.

And even when we do not face death, we should seek to live courageous lives in the day-to-day existence. C. S. Lewis once wrote, "Courage is not simply one of the virtues, but the form of every virtue at the testing point." So then, everyday courage is the ability to be honest when it is far more convenient to lie. It is the strength to speak the truth when the majority would prefer to hear something else.

Courage is the ability to resist the tantalizing apples of compromise when those around mock the "naïve" idea of right and wrong. It is standing firm in the face of the dragons of life who roar and pace and breath fire, snarling dark threats, who in the end cannot touch the essential: the immortal soul. Courage is the ability to meet our greatest fears and doubts and overcome them with the faith that says, "Though a thousand shall come against me, I will not fear, for You are with me."

When Elijah Lovejoy stood before the angry citizens of Alton, Illinois, the night of November 2, 1837, he refused to cease his anti-slavery writings and thereby compromise on what he knew to be right, even if it meant death at the hands of a mob. "You speak of compromise. But if by a compromise you mean for me to stop what duty requires of me, I will not do it! The reason is that I fear God more than man!" Courage in many ways proves God and all that He is; it shows the Lordship of Christ over the fear of man.

If we are afraid of giving up our wealth, our pensions, our comfortable lives because we fear what man might do to us, then we demonstrate through our actions that we fear man; that we rely more on man than on the Eternal Truth. Small compromises and acts of cowardice show a reliance on man instead of on God, and that we doubt Him who holds the destinies of all men and nations in His hands. We can never bring glory to God when being cowards in the face of fear.

When Nathan stood before David after David's adultery with Bathsheba, a lone man stood before the king of Israel, who with a word could have had Nathan killed. Yet Nathan, knowing he was sent by God, stood before David and said, "You are the man!" who had sinned before God. Nathan knew that he must ultimately please God, not the earthly king, and so found the courage to speak the inconvenient truth.

Because we are frail human beings, we will at times fail; we will retreat in fear when we should have met the challenge head on. We will take a bite of the apple of compromise and realize later that we played the fool. But we must show the courage to rise up from the failures and move on. We were made to glorify God, and when we show courage in the face of our fears, however big or small, we show that we believe; we believe that He is, and that ultimately it is God who we should seek to please and glorify.

For Christ and for His glory.

Becca, Nathaniel and Ned

STANDING FIRM

DREW RYUN

I believe that there are two different forms of courage. The first is physical courage, such as that of young American men scaling the cliffs of Normandy on June 6, 1944, or that of firemen and policemen rushing into the burning World Trade Towers on 9/11, or that of the passengers that rushed the hijackers on Flight 93 that same day. It is the ability to make snap decisions and run toward danger in spite of fear.

The second form of courage is the fortitude to go against the flow, like that of Micaiah in 1 Kings 22, or that of Joseph Warren, the great physician and orator in pre-American Revolution Boston, or that of William Wilberforce, the abolitionist statesman of nineteenth-century England. It is the ability to speak when no one else will, to have counted the cost well in advance and say to oneself, *If I don't say what needs to be said, no one else will.*

Micaiah stood before kings, countermanding the words of 400 other so-called prophets. Joseph Warren was the clarion voice of the American fight for Independence, giving what I consider one of the greatest speeches ever on March 5, 1775, in front of hostile British officers. I often wonder what Wilberforce felt in the moments leading up to his first speech against slavery on the floor of the British Parliament on May 12, 1789. Surely he had counted the cost. Did he know his advancing career was over? That the Yorkshire seat in the House of Commons was the last seat he would ever hold? That he would be vilified by the leading politicians of his day?

Our world is in short supply of this type of courage. I have lost count of how many times I have talked with others after political or policy meetings who've said to me, "I wish I had spoken up in there." I've lost count of how many times I've said that to myself.

So where does this courage of Micaiah, Warren and Wilberforce come from? I've thought a lot about it recently as we've written this book. I think it is because these were men who knew what they believed and knew without a shadow of a doubt that they were absolutely right in their beliefs. There is real strength in that, but it isn't something that happens overnight.

I think the first step to becoming a person of courage is to look in the mirror and ask yourself, *What do I believe?* The next is to take a piece of paper and write down an argument as to why you believe it. It is transforming to sit down and write the first sentence, "Why I am a Christian," and then on one sheet of paper explain the completeness of your worldview. On a parallel level is the connection of how this worldview impacts your political views and your relationships with your family and friends.

I think the second step to becoming a person of courage is to surround yourself with champions who are unafraid to challenge you. Proverbs 13:20 says, "He who walks with wise men will be wise," and in 1 Corinthians 15:33, the apostle Paul says, "Evil company corrupts good habits." While arguably the prophet Micaiah was a loner (1 Kings 22 does not mention much of his life), Warren and Wilberforce had a company of friends who were moving toward the same goals. Warren had his fellow Sons of Liberty, among who were men such as John Adams and Sam Adams. Wilberforce had his Clapham circle.

These were Warren and Wilberforce's companies of champions, many of them just as talented and as great as Warren and Wilberforce. The Warrens and Wilberforces believed, without a doubt, that they were right. And they placed themselves in a phalanx of like-minded champions. From this solid foundation of epistemology and mutual strength, they changed their worlds.

It has been said by some that had there been no Warren, there would have been no American War for Independence. Had there been no Wilberforce, slavery would have lasted much longer in England and the United States. Without a doubt, the courage of Wilberforce crossed the Atlantic to energize the American abolitionists.

Today, we live in a world of moral relativism that is antagonistic to our Christian worldview. If you choose to follow Christ, you will be called to daily acts of courage—some will be big; many will be small.

The time you take to lay the foundation for the future depends on you. Who you choose to surround yourselves with will impact the decisions you make. But believe me, there will be times when, like Micaiah, no one will stand with you.

Where then will you find the courage to stand firm?

Drew and Becca

MAKING THE SACRIFICE

JIM RYUN

Since the signing of the Declaration of Independence, millions of men and women have fought for the freedom and independence we cherish today. While the sacrifice has been great, its fruits have been many. As Thomas Paine once said, "Those who expect to reap the blessings of freedom, must, like men, undergo the fatigues of supporting it."

Each year, on Memorial Day, we have the privilege of honoring the men and women who took Thomas Paine's words to heart and sacrificed their lives for the advancement of freedom—freedom not just in America, but throughout the entire world.

Memorial Day 2006 held special significance as we honored the men and women who sacrificed during the Second World War by dedicating the World War II Memorial in Washington, D.C. Throughout that war, America stood united. Men and women, both on the front lines in Europe and on the assembly lines in the United States, changed a broken world imperiled by dictators into a world of free nations rebuilding toward new opportunities.

September 2, 1945, marked the official end of World War II, but the contributions of our soldiers continue to this day. As a result of Harry Colmery's work in drafting the original GI Bill in 1943, millions of soldiers returned to America where they received an education and job training. The result was an American workforce enriched by 450,000 engineers, 238,000 teachers, 91,000 scientists, 67,000 doctors, 22,000 dentists, and more than one million other college-educated men and women. The modern middle class was born and everyone today has benefited from its contributions.

Unfortunately, as I write these words, the freedom our World War II veterans fought for is again under attack.

We know all too well the devastating reality of a terrorist attack on our freedom. The War on Terror has now led us to Iraq where we are making great strides towards freedom and security. Because of growing economic stability, new businesses are opening throughout the country. Iraqis are enjoying electricity and clean drinking water. Schools and hospitals are reopening.

While some have criticized our soldiers, I am very proud of their great service and determination. I have had the honor of spending time with these men and women, seeing firsthand the strong character with which the vast majority serves our country. As a result of their sacrifice, Iraq is transitioning from a ruthless, authoritative regime to a free and democratic nation. Our cause is just and right. As in World War II, we will not rest until our mission is complete.

We are taught to do justly, to love mercy, and to walk humbly with our God. It is these principles that allow America to stand strong in the face of adversity.

Each year on Memorial Day, take time to thank a veteran for their sacrifice and service. Also, I urge each one of you to pray daily for our troops serving bravely around the world.

As a family, we get together as often as possible. Sometimes, I even let Drew and Ned beat me when playing golf. Here we relax in Purcellville, Virginia, in the Spring of 2006. From left to right: Becca Ryun, Ned Ryun, Catharine Ryun, Anne Ryun, Nathaniel Ryun, Jim Ryun, Drew Ryun, Becca Ryun.

ENDNOTES

Day 3: Justice and Mercy

1. *The Complete Works of Shakespeare*, New York, 1975, Random House Value Publishing, p. 222.

Day 5: A Reasonable Faith

1. A. W. Tozer, *The Pursuit of God* (Camp Hill, PA: Christian Publications, Inc, 1982), p. 53.

Day 8: Tough Decisions

1. Wilberforce, William. *The Speech of William Wilberforce, Esq., Representative for the County of York, On the Question of the Abolition of the Slave Trade.* London: 1789. This edition of the speech edited by Kevin Belmonte, Director of The Wilberforce Project, Gordon College.

Day 9: Integrity

1. Thomas McKean of Delaware would sign the document in January of 1777.
2. Joseph J. Ellis, *Founding Brothers* (New York: Vintage Books, 2002), n.p.

Day 12: His Pleasure

1. Hugh Hudson, dir., *Chariots of Fire* (Los Angeles: Warner Brothers, 1981).

Day 14: God Is

1. C.S. Lewis, *The Lion, the Witch and the Wardrobe (The Chronicles of Narnia)* (New York: HarperCollins, 2005), n.p.

Day 19

1. J. T. Headley, *Chaplains and Clergy of the Revolution* (New York: C. Scribner and Sons, 1864), p. 227.

Day 23: Necessary Failure

1. Herman Melville, quoted in *The Piazza Tales and Other Prose Pieces 1839-1860, The Writings of Herman Melville, vol. 9,* Harrison Hayford, Alma A. MacDougall and G. Thomas Tanselle, eds. (Evanston, IL: Northwestern University Press, 1987), n.p.

Day 24: Pure Gold

1. John Foxe, Foxe's Christian Martyrs of the World (San Antonio, TX: Mantle Ministries), p. 468.
2. Ibid.

Day 26: Awakenings

1. Francis Schaeffer. *A Christian Manifesto* (Wheaton, IL: Crossway Books, 1982), p. 78.

Day 27: Here Today

1. Francis Wayland, *A Memoir of the Life and Labors of the Rev. Adoniram Judson, D.D.* (Boston, MA: Phillips, Sampson and Company, 1853), vol. 1, p. 33.

Day 28: Powerhouse of Prayer

1. C.H. Spurgeon, quoted in David Smithers, "Charles H. Spurgeon: Prayer Makes History," Revival Resource Center. http://www.watchword.org/smithers/ww40a.html (accessed June 20, 2006).
2. Larry J. Michael, Ph.D., "Spurgeon and the Power of Prayer," Martin Roth Christian Commentary. http://www.martinrothonline.com/ChristianLiving/spurgeon.htm (accessed June 20, 2006).

Day 31: Superman

1. Tommy Walker, "He Knows My Name," © Doulos Publishing, 1996.

Day 46: A Successful Life

1. Marcus L. Loane, *Makers of Religious Freedom in the 17th Century* (Grand Rapids, MI: William B. Eerdmans Publishing Co., 1961), p. 61.
2. Ibid, p. 101.
3. Ibid.
4. Ibid, p.102.

Day 47: A Life of Giving

1. A. W. Tozer, *The Pursuit of God* (CampHill, PA: Christian Publications, 1993), p. 27.

Day 48: Like a Dash

1. François Fenélon, *Let Go* (Kensington, PA: Whitaker House, 1973), p. 47.
2. Ibid. n.p.

Day 57: A Sovereign God

1. William J. Bryan, *The World's Famous Orations* (New York: Funk and Wagnalls Company, 1906), vol. 8, pp. 110-122.
2. Lewis Henry Boutell, *The Life of Roger Sherman* (Chicago: A.C. McClure and Company, 1896), pp. 272-273.

About Jim Ryun

Jim Ryun is serving his fifth term in Congress, representing the Second Congressional District of Kansas. He is a member of the Armed Services, Budget and Financial Services Committees. Jim continues to promote a message of economic relief for the families of the Second District, working to ease the tax burden and eliminate unnecessary governmental regulations. As a citizen-statesman, Jim serves the people with a commitment to honesty and integrity.

Jim was the founder and president of Jim Ryun Sports, Inc., a public relations company. Through this company, Jim traveled across the country acting as a product development consultant, marketing products and promoting awareness of various charities. Immediately prior to serving in Congress, Jim partnered with the ReSound Hearing Aid Company, creating his own program "Sounds of Success," aimed at helping-hearing impaired children fulfill their potential.

Married in January of 1969, Jim and Anne Ryun live in Lawrence, Kansas. They have four adult children: Heather, Ned, Drew and Catharine. Heather and Captain Daymen Tiffany were married on October 26, 1997, and have three children: Justus Nathaniel (born January 21, 1999), Walker Leon (January 19, 2001) and Mercedes Anne (May 28, 2003) Tiffany. Drew and Rebecca Anne Douglas were married on December 4, 2004. Ned and Rebecca Anne Parker were married on February 5, 2005, and have one child: Nathaniel Charles Jr. (born February 5, 2006).

Jim achieved national acclaim as a track and field star while a high school student in Wichita. In 1965, Jim set the male High School Mile Record of 3:55.3—a record that stood for 36 years. Jim participated in three summer Olympic games in 1964, 1968 and 1972, winning a silver medal in the 1,500-meter run in 1968. Jim also held the World Record in the mile, 1,500 meters and 880 yards.

MILESTONES

April 29, 1947: Born in Wichita, Kansas.

June 5, 1964: Becomes the first high school student to break the 4-minute mile, running 3:59.0.

September 1964: Makes first Olympic team at the 1,500-meter, representing the United States at the Tokyo Olympics.

June 27, 1965: Wins AAU championships and sets the American record for the mile at 3:55.3, which stood as the high school record for 36 years.

June 10, 1966: Runs 1:44.9 for the 880-meter at Terre Haute, Indiana, setting the World Record.

July 8, 1966: Wins the 1,500-meter at the Commonwealth versus United States track and field meet in Los Angeles, California, setting a new World Record of 3:33.1.

July 17, 1966: Wins the mile at the United States All Comers meet in Berkeley, California, setting a new World Record of 3:51.3. Ranked first in the world for 1966 in the mile and 800-meter by *Track and Field News*. Also named World Track and Field Athlete of the Year by *Track and Field News*.

February 25, 1967: Named the James A. Sullivan Amateur Athlete of the Year for 1966. Named by *Sports Illustrated* as Sportsman of the Year for 1966.

June 23, 1967: Wins the AAU mile at Bakersfield, California, setting a new World Record of 3:51.1. Ranked the number one miler in the world for 1967 by *Track and Field News*. Also named World Track and Field Athlete of the Year.

September 1968:	Makes second Olympic team at the 1,500-meter, winning the 1968 Olympic Trials in Lake Tahoe, California.
October 1968:	Wins the silver medal in the 1,500-meter final at the 1968 Mexico City Olympics.
January 25, 1969:	Marries Anne Snider at Bay Village, Ohio.
June 21, 1970:	First daughter, Heather DeKlyn Ryun (now Tiffany) is born in Topeka, Kansas.
May 18, 1972:	Accepts Christ as Lord and Savior.
July 1972:	Makes third Olympic team at 1,500-meter.
July 29, 1972:	Runs the third-fastest mile of all time, 3:52.8, at the Metro Toronto Police Games in Toronto, California.
September 1972:	Represents the United States in the 1,500-meter at the Munich Olympic Games, his last Olympics.
February 28, 1973:	Twin sons Nathaniel (Ned) Charles Ryun and Andrew (Drew) Monroe Ryun are born in Santa Barbara, California.
April 1975:	Starts the Jim Ryun Running Camps.
July 26, 1975:	Birth of second daughter, Catharine Anne Ryun, in Santa Barbara, California.
August 1981:	Moves from Santa Barbara, California, to Lawrence, Kansas.
1984:	*In Quest of Gold,* written by Jim Ryun and Michael Phillips, is published by Harper and Row.
November 1996:	Elected as Congressman for the Second District of Kansas.
1998:	Re-elected for second term as Congressman.
2000:	Re-elected for third term as Congressman.
2002:	Re-elected for fourth term as Congressman.
2002:	*Heroes Among Us,* written by Jim Ryun and Sons, is published by Destiny Image. Re-elected for fourth term as Congressman.
June 12, 2003:	Cosponsored House Resolution 2444 (the Parents' Right to Know Act).

2003:	Inducted into the National Distance Running Hall of Fame.
May 9, 2003:	Cosponsored House Resolution 2045, the Ten Commandments Defense Act.
2004:	Re-elected for fifth term as Congressman.
March 2, 2005:	Cosponsored House Resolution 1100, the Marriage Protection Act.
April 21, 2005:	Cosponsored House Resolution 1804, to prescribe the oath of renunciation and allegiance for purposes of the Immigration and Nationality Act.
September 14, 2005:	Sponsored House Resolution 3132 Amendment to appeal the decision in United States v. Helder, Jr. and aggressively continue to track down and prosecute sex offenders on the Internet.
May 2, 2006:	Sponsored House Resolution 793, affirming that statements of national unity, including the National Anthem, should be recited or sung in English.
2006:	Currently sits as member on the House Armed Services, Financial Services and Budget Committees. Since 1996, Jim has introduced or cosponsored 527 bills in Congress.

Here I accept the *Sports Illustrated* Sportsman of the Year Award. It was the Spring of 1967 in New York City. What a great honor for a boy from Kansas!

ACKNOWLEDGMENTS

It is impossible to list everyone who has impacted my life in some small way, but there have been many. Nothing in my life has been achieved without the support and encouragement of numerous people who have deeply enriched my life and helped make me who I am today.

To Christ, who loved me before I even knew Him. Without Him, I would be nothing. To my parents, Gerald and Wilma, who both have gone to be with Christ. To my in-laws, Moose and Betty Snider, who gave us immeasurable support amid some of life's challenges. To my wife, Anne, who from the night we met on a blind date in 1967 has been my greatest cheerleader. Without her love and support, I could not be where I am today. To my children, Heather, Ned, Drew and Catharine, who have been all that I could have ever hoped for in sons and daughters. They have in so many ways made me very proud.

To my son-in-law, Daymen, and my daughters-in-law, the Beccas, who have become like a son and daughters to me. To my grandchildren, Justus, Walker, Mercedes and Nathaniel, who always bring a smile to Grampie's face. To my coach, Bob (Timmie) Timmons, who inspired a skinny, awkward, unsure high school boy to take the first step in a great adventure and helped me see beyond the present and dream of what could be. To his wife, Pat (Pat-Pat), who cheered me on in hundreds of races and many times fed and cared for me as I pursued Olympic glory. To Neal Steinhauer and others who faithfully sowed the seeds of Christ in my life, and to Bernie and Clara Taylor, who helped bring those seeds to fruition.

In regard to this book, I want to thank Bill Denzel and Roger Thompson, who sat with Ned, Drew and me and proposed a book project. To Ned and Drew, who took my thoughts and life-lessons and put them onto paper. Without their writing and hard work, this book would never have happened. To Steve Lawson, Deena Davis, Mark Weising, Rob Williams and the rest of the team at Regal. Finally, to Rich Clarkson, whose amazing photography chronicled my career from high school to my days on the pro circuit.

YOU CAN CONTACT JIM RYUN AT

Jim Ryun
Washington, D.C.
1110 Longworth HOB
Washington, D.C. 20515
(202) 225-6601
http://ryun.house.gov/

Go One-on-One with Sports Legends

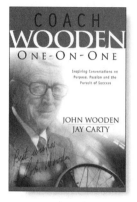
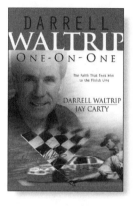
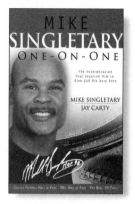
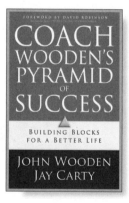
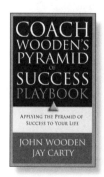

God's Word for Your World

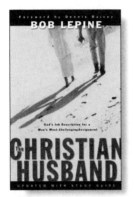

The Christian Husband
God's Job Description for a Man's
Most Challenging Assignment
Bob Lepine
ISBN 08307.36891

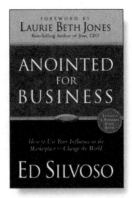

Anointed for Business
How Christians Can Use Their
Influence in the Marketplace
to Change the World
Ed Silvoso
ISBN 08307.41968

Living Life Boldly
No Regrets, No What-Ifs—
Selling Out to What Really Matters
Ted Roberts
ISBN 08307.31083

**The Five Secrets to
Becoming a Leader**
Words of Wisdom for
the Untrained Leader
Alan Nelson and *Stan Toler*
ISBN 08307.29151

**Moments Together
for Couples**
Daily Devotions for Drawing Near
to God and One Another
Dennis and Barbara Rainey
ISBN 08307.17544

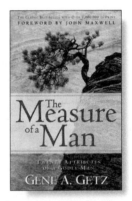

The Measure of a Man
Twenty Attributes of a Godly Man
Gene A. Getz
ISBN 08307.34953